Speaking of Children

The Singapore Children's Society
Collected Lectures

Speaking of

Children

The Singapore Children's Society
Collected Lectures

World Scientific

NEW JERSEY • LONDON • SINGAPORE • BEIJING • SHANGHAI • HONG KONG • TAIPEI • CHENNAI • TOKYO

Published by

World Scientific Publishing Co. Pte. Ltd.
5 Toh Tuck Link, Singapore 596224
USA office: 27 Warren Street, Suite 401-402, Hackensack, NJ 07601
UK office: 57 Shelton Street, Covent Garden, London WC2H 9HE

Library of Congress Cataloging-in-Publication Data
Speaking of children : the Singapore Children's Society collected lectures / Singapore Children's
Society.
      pages cm
    Includes index.
    ISBN 978-9814699273 (pbk. : alk. paper)
    1. Children--Singapore. 2. Singapore--Social conditions. 3. Families--Singapore. I. Balakrishnan,
Vivian. Children. Container of (work): II. Singapore Children's Society.
    HQ792.S55S64 2015
    305.23095957--dc23

                                                    2015020386

British Library Cataloguing-in-Publication Data
A catalogue record for this book is available from the British Library.

In-house Editor: Qi Xiao

Typeset by Stallion Press
Email: enquiries@stallionpress.com

In the 50th Anniversary Year
of the Independence of Singapore

This book is

Dedicated

To the Children of Singapore

and

In memory of Lee Kuan Yew (1923–2015)

who gave them the fruits of that Independence

Foreword

Civilisation has progressed to the age of digital technology, but everywhere children remain exposed and vulnerable. Many are without their natural protectors — parents and family — so we cannot count ourselves civilised if we leave such children to their plight, caught between poverty and predators.

We are all, at the same time, trustees of this earth and duty-bound to preserve it — its beauty and resources for the benefit of all the children of the world. The obligations we owe to the children of the world are interwoven with our responsibility to safeguard the earth itself. Both causes will be futile if we were to ignore either of them. It is our obligation to bring up children healthy in mind and body, and educate them to cherish the earth as we do so that they may grow up to be responsible trustees to the children that come after them. That has to be the continuing legacy of the human race.

This book's collection of lectures is of immense value, not just because it serves as a record of the efforts of the past, a reminder of the present and an inspiration for the future, it also pricks the conscience and rouses our protective instinct which sometimes tends to be in slumber, and at other times appears numbed by the distractions of life. This book is a call to awakening.

Justice Choo Han Teck
Supreme Court, Singapore

Preface

This book collects together eight lectures, one for each year since the Singapore Children's Society inaugurated its annual lecture series in 2007. Each speaker selected their own topic, but by the time six or seven lectures had been delivered, it was apparent that there were certain common themes emerging. When the lectures were initiated, we did not anticipate publishing them, but happily all eight speakers later gave their consent for the publication of their lectures, and taken together they constitute an interesting set of reflections.

Historically, childhood has seen a transformation in Singapore in the decades since independence. This has been reflected in the changing needs of children and the changing focus of the Society's contribution. As this transformation occurred under post-independence PAP governments, it is fitting that Chapter One provides a historical perspective on children, provided by a member of the Government, starting with reflections on the impact our children have on our lives, and why they are and have always been such an important element in our society. Some of the telling facts and figures that are indispensable to politicians are there, to buttress an overview of the development of a legislative and administrative framework that can serve the needs and wishes of children and their families; but this is also a personal account, written by one, Vivian Balakrishnan, who is himself the product, and still youthful beneficiary, of the history he describes.

Chapter Two also provides a historical perspective but in this case a focussed and highly personal account by a very senior social worker. Ann Wee is better qualified than almost any other person, to comment from the perspective of one who has married and made a career in social work in Singapore. She has a host of unique experiences to call to her aid. By using the Chinese family as her example, she speaks from personal as much as from professional experience, yet her message is pure Singapore and will surely resonate deeply with Singaporeans of all races. It is particularly perceptive, perhaps, in contrasting Confucian and western attitudes to family, and in discussing continuities in our local attitudes to family matters despite the huge changes wrought by health, wealth and education.

There are many matters concerning children that are liable to create unease in the older generation. One of the most potent is the threat, or promise, and certainly the fact, of greater economic and sexual freedom that has tended to come with modernisation. Our laws make assumptions about the nature of maturity and coming of age, and they thereby also create anomalies. As a former Attorney-General, and the only Nominated MP ever to originate a parliamentary Bill, Walter Woon expertly guided his fascinated audience — in his original talk — through some of these anomalies and the legal and ethical problems they create and, sometimes, fail to solve. His observations in Chapter Three are increasingly relevant in today's world, where concerns about the nature of internet freedoms and the safety of children online are a concern of many.

Sexual maturity brings specific issues to the fore, but in fact there is a general and ongoing interest in contrasts across the generations. What used to be called simply the generation gap — whatever it really was — has given way to more detailed consideration of a whole succession of specifiable generations — Generations

X, Y, Z and, before them, the Baby Boomers. Aline Wong — speaking as an academic more than as the politician she once was — casts in Chapter Four a sociologist's eye on the phenomena of generational characteristics and differences, and what they mean for today's generations. Interestingly, she notes both the convergences between local and western youth, and the areas where differences remain, despite pervasive globalisation.

It takes an entrepreneur, perhaps, to tackle issues while at the same time professing no formal knowledge of the subject. Thus Ho Kwon Ping (Chapter Five) disarmingly claims a lack of qualification, and then discourses effectively on parenting and his experiences in the University of Life, which would seem to have prepared him better than most for life as it is actually lived. His advice is especially valuable for parents. Parenting is something you learn on the job. Books, in-laws, and other relatives and friends are no substitute for the real thing; but every little bit you can glean from others who have been there, and survived, and flourished, and who share their thinking, is valuable.

Chapter Six addresses another issue close to the heart of many parents — that of discipline. To cane, or not to cane, that is the question. Singaporean parents tend to cane; but Leong Wai Kum, a lawyer and academic, does not think the practice is defensible. In the course of a review of family law in Singapore, she adds a voice of internal dissent to a chorus of international disapproval. In fact, the issue is not as straightforward as sometimes thought, on both sides of the debate, as the research suggests cultural context has an important bearing on the outcome of disciplinary practices. Nonetheless, it is increasingly hard to maintain the position, beloved of an earlier generation, that sparing the rod really spoils the child.

Chapter Seven is very modern, and it addresses family issues. The Speaker of Parliament, Halimah Yacob, knows better than most the challenges of reconciling children, a family and a career. It is a challenge faced by every working parent, though as

Mdm Halimah pointedly notes, questions of coping tend to be asked only of women. No one, she comments, asks her male parliamentary colleagues how *they* cope with combining marriage and a career. Changes in the workplace and in the family have not yet extended to making the former sufficiently compatible with the needs of the latter, and the Speaker had suggestions as to what might be done here.

Chapter Eight, the last in this volume, is one that takes us in an unexpected and literary direction. Taking his cue from the Lebanese poet, the late Kahlil Gibran, Janadas Devan takes the famous first line of Gibran's poem On Children — "Your children are not your children" — and embeds it in modern times. Parents in general, but Asian parents especially, are well known for their desire to give their children a good start in life. It is common for members of the older generation to bemoan the passing of childhoods like their own, a vanished golden age, in which children could play outdoors, run free, and were less pressured academically. Such reminiscences may gild the lily, and overlook the downside of childhood in less developed societies, but it is true that today's child is all too often burdened with the combined weight of parental expectations and filial obligations. For Janadas, who also draws freely on his own and his parents' lives and experiences, it is not realistic to suppose that parents can be controlling in a modern world. They cannot foresee the destinations their children will reach. As the poet puts it, our children are our arrows to the future, and of the archer he writes, "For even as He loves the arrow that flies, so He loves also the bow that is stable." Parents can and should provide stable foundations, but they also need to let go.

Taken together, these chapters represent a series of thoughtful essays, originally delivered as fascinating public lectures, and now recast as a set of related chapters in a book on children and families. For 63 years, the Children's Society has addressed the welfare of children in need. In the 1950s and 1960s that need was often basic nutrition and care. Then, it shifted to become focussed on problems of child maltreatment, or lonely children, or latch-key children. It became concerned with families and set up a family service centre. But underlying these charitable works was the assumption that most children are not in need.

However, a theme running through the chapters in this book is the importance of values; and values are something that affect us all. For example, rather than just consider children who are abused, we need to consider the entire question of whether or not corporal punishment should be evaluated as a kind of abuse. Rather than worry only about children who are delinquent, or neglected, or beyond parental control, we have to think of what fundamental values we would like to inculcate in all our children, and how best to partition the responsibilities of families and the state. Rather than think only about particular needy children who have not been well served by society as it is, we also need to think about how society should treat all its children generally. We need to move from the particular to the general. In other words, we need to consider not just children with specific needs, but what makes for a better foundation and provision for all our children. Children are not a species apart. Few parents, in these days of small families, really think any longer that their children should be seen and not heard. The adults who speak most warmly of their own parents tend to be those who enjoyed a family life in which there was some give and take. Maybe it is time for children's voices to be heard and for the Children's Society to help give them that voice.

The lectures on which these chapters are based are an ongoing project. There will be more speakers and more lectures as time goes on, for the task of keeping abreast of change never ends. But the present contributors have thought long and deeply about the issues they address. Their lectures were received with much appreciation, and the many questions asked revealed the interest sparked in their audience. To each lecture we have added an introduction — About the Speaker — and a specially commissioned cartoon by Morgan Chua. We have also incorporated into most of them excerpts from the question and answer sessions. In the interest of bringing these speakers' thoughts to a wider audience, in a more permanent form, this volume is now offered to the public.

This book also celebrates 50 years of independence. When Raffles, an employee of the East India Company, founded modern Singapore, the idea of independence would have been an utterly strange one to him. Yet, since independence, Raffles has been maintained as a symbol of Singapore, as a unifying figure, and his vision in seeing the strategic potential of Singapore is well recognised. The speakers in these lectures were children once, and perhaps it is not too fanciful to suppose that were Raffles to see them today, as the realisation of what Singapore has become in the last 50 years, he would be proud of them and what they represent. In the fullness of time and with the mature judgement of history, Raffles may be replaced in the public mind by Lee Kuan Yew, as the man who — with his lieutenants — founded independent Singapore as we know it today. We hope that he, too, would have felt some measure of pride and approval, of the effort to give meaning to independence that these lectures represent, and we dedicate this volume to his memory in that hope.

Koh Choon Hui
Chairman, Singapore Children's Society

The Speakers as Children of Singapore

Acknowledgements

The book came to fruition with the support and contribution of many parties. The Book Committee would like to express our gratitude to:

The Speakers, for generously sharing their post-lecture reflections, reviewing their lecture transcripts, and contributing their childhood photos. To their personal assistants and secretaries, thank you for putting up with our constant hounding.

Morgan Chua, for translating our ideas into illustrative cartoons. His little bull worked very hard to please this fastidious committee.

Geraldine Tan, Tan Lee Lee, Toh Pei Yi and Sheryl Tan, for their hard work in transcribing the Q&A segments of the lectures.

LexisNexis Singapore and Yong Teck Meng, for granting us the free use of their material to illustrate the book. We are also appreciative of the cartoons by Chew and Miel made available by *The Straits Times*.

About
Singapore Children's Society
and
the Lectures

Singapore Children's Society protects and nurtures children and youth of all races and religions. In 2014, the Society reached out to 68,292 children, youth and families in need. Established in 1952, its services have evolved to meet the changing needs of children. Today, Children's Society operates 10 service centres island-wide, offering services in four categories: Vulnerable Children Services, Children and Youth Services, Family Services and Research and Advocacy.

The annual Singapore Children's Society Lecture, inaugurated in 2007 as part of our 55th Anniversary Celebrations, is one of the Society's efforts to reach out to professionals working with children and families as well as to the members of the public. Each Lecture, during which a subject expert speaks on a topic related to children, aims to raise public awareness on an issue pertinent to the welfare and wellbeing of children, youth and families.

Contents

CHAPTER ONE

Children — Our Hope and Future

Vivian Balakrishnan

About the Speaker

Dr Vivian Balakrishnan has been a Member of Parliament since 2001. At the time of his lecture he was Minister for Community Development, Youth and Sports (MCYS) and Second Minister for Information, Communication and the Arts. He was subsequently appointed the Minister for the Environment and Water Resources.

Dr Balakrishnan studied Medicine at the National University of Singapore after being awarded a President's Scholarship in 1980. He was elected President of the NUS Students' Union Council from 1981 to 1983 and Chairman from 1984 to 1985. After graduation, he specialised in Ophthalmology. He was appointed Associate Professor at NUS and Deputy Director of the Singapore National Eye Centre (SNEC) in 1997. He led several clinical research trials to control the progression of myopia in children and in 1999 became the Medical Director of SNEC. He was appointed Chief Executive Officer of the Singapore General Hospital in 2000.

He was also made Minister-in-charge of the Smart Nation initiative. He previously held appointments as Second Minister for Trade and Industry, Minister responsible for Entrepreneurship and Minister of State for National Development. During the early years of his political career, he served as Chairman of the "Remaking Singapore" committee and Chairman of the National Youth Council. He also served two terms as Chairman of the Young PAP.

In Parliament, he has been active with new legislation or amendments to existing legislation with a bearing on children's welfare. These include the Community Care Endowment Fund Act, the International Child Abduction Act, and amendments to the Child Development Co-Savings Act, the Children and Young Persons Act and the Women's Charter.

In a similar vein, whilst at the then MCYS, Dr Balakrishnan oversaw the establishment of the ComCare Endowment Fund and refinement of the ComCare Social Assistance framework; the Enabling Masterplan for persons with disability; the establishment of the Central Youth Guidance Office; and the expansion of Family Service Centres and the Accreditation of Social Workers. He has also led the upgrading of the childcare sector and the establishment of the National Family Council, Charities Council, Community Foundation of Singapore, National Steering Committee on Racial and Religious Harmony, the National Integration Council, the Council for Third Age and the National Council against Problem Gambling. He supervised the successful hosting of the inaugural Youth Olympic Games in 2010; and the redevelopment of the National Stadium. This list by no means exhausts Dr Balakrishnan's legislative and ministerial activities.

The Children's Society book committee members met the Minister in 2014 and asked him for his reflections, given that seven years had elapsed since his lecture, and that this book would be published in the 50th year of independence. Dr Balakrishnan highlighted what had been done in the period since, such as the support for early childhood education, the moves to make court cases involving the Family Court and juvenile justice less adversarial, and the reduction of emphasis on streaming in school. Nonetheless, he felt he would still say much the same in a lecture now as he said in 2007, as his remarks would still be applicable.

The Minister's commitment to family life and his fond recollections of his own parents and grandparents, especially his mother and grand-mother, were obvious. He was specific on the importance he person-ally attached to making sure he was there for his own children, taking them to school, seeing them in the evening and eating together at meals. On Sundays, whenever possible, family members visit his father who is 84. He has been married for 27 years to his wife, Joy. He was glad that the divorce rate seems to have stabilised at around seven per 1000, but was concerned nonetheless that some 6,000 children annually go through the stress of their parents' separation or divorce. A child, he felt, needs a father and a mother, and in his view a father's gift to his children is to love their mother. Children need the security of knowing this.

Dr Balakrishnan gave credit to Singapore Children's Society for its role in pursuing the welfare of all children. He saw the Society as occupying a certain moral high ground through being a voluntary organisation, and thus able to press for children's needs in an impartial and credible way. He supported the Society's focus on the future of children and its efforts to move into a new phase that would address the needs and hear the voices of children, urging that all the lectures in the series, and not just his own, be seen as a means of fur-thering the work of the Society.

A much younger Vivian Balakrishnan with his parents

The 1st Lecture, delivered 28 September 2007

I am delighted to be here with you this evening to deliver the Singapore Children's Society Inaugural Lecture and to be a part of the Singapore Children's Society's 55th Anniversary celebrations. Today, the Society stands as a premier child-focussed organisation, serving some 12,000 children through your 10 service centres. I commend you for your unwavering commitment to the welfare of our children over the past 55 years.

Introduction

The first question to ask ourselves is: Why children? Why are they so important to us? I would like to suggest that the answer lies in understanding the impact of children on our lives and on society. Imagine, if you will, a society with immortal adults and no children. My guess is that such a society would be tired, stale, cautious, hedonistic and perhaps one where people have nothing to live for except themselves. On the other hand, children represent new possibilities, new hopes, rejuvenation, vitality, fearlessness and optimism. A society with many children is one that believes in the future and will invest in the future.

On the night my daughter was born, I discovered the meaning of unconditional parental love and total responsibility for a new life. I realised how much my parents had loved me, how I could never repay them. I finally understood why family ties are the fundamental bedrock of human society. This is the real reason we encourage people to marry and have children. It is not economics that is our primary concern. The tone and outlook of our society is of far greater importance.

Setting the Context — Strategic Trends Shaping Child Development

Since our independence, the context in which our children grow up has changed dramatically. Let me offer you a snapshot of what I mean. Between 1965 and 2006, Singapore's per capita Gross Domestic Product grew from $1,580 to $53,355. Taking a more recent comparison, the median household income of families has risen by close to 100 percent, from $2,296 in 1990 to $4,500 in 2006.[1] Our prosperity has ensured that children today are free from many of the daily struggles that earlier generations faced. Today, most families enjoy — and are able to provide their children with — a standard of living vastly better than that of a generation or two before.

Another key driver shaping our children's environment is technology. Emails have replaced hard-copy memos and snazzy multimedia presentations have replaced the trusted transparency! Many of our children today would scoff at the difficulties we faced in making the transition to today's high-tech world. This is because the majority of them are digital natives. In 2006, 78 percent of households in Singapore had access to one or more computers at home. Seventy-one percent also had access to the internet. Our children are learning early that they can access YouTube to watch their favourite cartoons rather than wait for them to air on television.

The rise of single parenthood in this generation illuminates the changing face of family life over the centuries and the inextricable link between economic development and family form. Early agrarian society was characterised by extended families who worked the farms collectively and shared responsibility for the care of the children. The Industrial Revolution resulted in urbanisation and the phenomenon of nuclear families living in the city without the support of the extended family. Fathers worked and mothers were expected to stay at home. Between 1980 and 2006, in Singapore, the general divorce rate for women rose from

---

[1] In 2014 the GDP per capita was $71,318 and median household income was $8,290. *Key Household Income Trends, 2014*, Singapore Department of Statistics, http://www. singstat.gov.sg/docs/default-source/default-document-library/publications/publications_and_papers/household_income_and_expenditure/pp-s21.pdf. Accessed 26 June 2015.

3.8 to 7.4 for every 1,000 married resident females.[2] In 1990, about 8.6 percent of resident households with at least one child below 16 years were headed by single parents. In 2005, this proportion fell slightly to 6.8 percent. Despite the parents' best intentions, these families are more likely to struggle to provide the best home and future for their children.

Source: *The Straits Times* © Singapore Press Holdings Limited. Reprinted with permission.

The key question for all of us today is what impact the post-modern world is likely to have on family life. The sociological impacts are likely to be as profound as the earlier revolutions. As early as the seventies, American academic Edward Shorter[3] noted three key traits of the post-modern family, to which I am sure we can relate.

First, adolescent indifference to the family's identity and a corresponding identification with other networks and their peers. Second, instability in the lives of couples. The divorce rates I have just mentioned are one manifestation. Finally, the end of the notion of a "nest" in nuclear family life, with the liberation of women. As more women enter the workforce, fewer children now return to homes with mums awaiting their return.

---

[2] It has remained at about this level subsequently, for example it was 6.9 in 2013. *Population Trends 2014*, Singapore Department of Statistics, http://www.singstat.gov.sg/docs/default-source/default-document-library/publications/publications_and_papers/population_and_population_structure/population2014.pdf-title=Statistics. Accessed 26 June 2015.

[3] Edward Shorter, *The Making of the Modern Family* (New York: Basic Press, 1975).

Another feature of the post-modern family is susceptibility to a myriad of influences, including electronic media. Our children grow up with MapleStory and World of Warcraft where they lead virtual lives and belong to virtual tribes. They are well versed in the applications of YouTube for viewing all kinds of videos beyond censorship or supervision. And they are well entrenched in the worlds of MySpace, Friendster and Facebook which provide them with platforms to mingle and catch up with their friends without having to leave their homes.

What does this mean for the "post-modern" child, so to speak? It means living in a world of abundant choices whilst being bombarded by unlimited temptations and influences. It means the richness of participating in multiple communities, whilst struggling to find one's core identity and values. It means the opportunity to chart new frontiers but sometimes without the clear guidance of a moral compass.

The complexities of the world would also mean that children who are more well-off may face one too many choices or temptations, whilst children who are less well-off may miss out on opportunities that the post-modern world offers. Consequently, we need to take stock and paint a comprehensive vision of what we want to achieve for Singapore's children.

Articulating a Shared Vision for Children

As part of the 10th anniversary celebrations to commemorate Singapore's accession to the UN Convention on the Rights of the Child, my Ministry (MCYS) launched a postcard campaign in 2006. We invited children to share their aspirations. It has been a wonderful reality check for me and my staff to hear them. Their views collectively articulate a shared vision for children and point us to what we need to do to create a child-friendly Singapore. A Singapore that allows them to feel a sense of belonging, to participate, to be protected from harm and to fulfil their potential. It is only appropriate that their voices frame our discussion of the key priorities and on-going efforts in developing children.

Promoting Health

> "My wish for children in Singapore is for them to be healthy and good so that children will not be ill and die."— Matthew Foo, 9

> "My wish for children in Singapore is for every child to be happy and healthy and for every day to be a jubilant and joyful day. May they smile every day of their life." — Lee Xinyi, 13

Gro Brundtland, former Director-General of the World Health Organisation, once said that "Health is the core of human development." As a medical doctor myself, I could not agree more. Children in Singapore enjoy accessible, high-quality and equitable healthcare. In 2005, the infant mortality rate was 2.1 per 1,000 live births, compared to 26.3 per 1,000 live births in 1965. Our infant mortality rate was ranked by UNICEF's *State of the World's Children Report* in 2005 and 2006 as the best in the world. This dramatic improvement is attributable to improvements in obstetric care, and advances in medical care, especially in new-born care in Singapore.

Today, a robust health screening programme is in place for the young. Annually, about 99 percent of 7- and 12-year-olds are screened for abnormal hearing, visual acuity and heart conditions, and provided with growth and developmental assessment in schools. Children identified with health problems are referred to relevant healthcare institutions for further evaluation and management at the primary, secondary and tertiary care levels.

Health, of course, is not just about the absence of illness, disease, or injury. It is also about general wellbeing. The mental health issues of children and adolescents are slowly gaining prominence. It is an area that we must understand better and tackle in a more holistic manner.

Providing Quality Education

> "My wish for children in Singapore is for each child to be able to pursue education so that they can develop their potential to the fullest and make Singapore a better place for everyone."
> — Ainsley Le, 14

Let me move on to the area of education. The challenge is to impart to our children the values, skills and knowledge needed to thrive in a rapidly changing world. Education remains the key enabler and it is a resource-intensive endeavour. Today, the government invests about $6.5 billion in education — about 3.5 percent of our GDP.

Our priority for all children is to get them to schools in the first instance. A cornerstone of this effort is our compulsory education policy for primary school education, in place since 2003. The Singapore Children's Society is familiar with this, being actively involved in outreach to children who truant or who do not even get registered for school.

For those who are already in schools, our priority is to keep them in our system for as long as we can. Northlight School, set up in 2006, embodies this effort. Northlight's mandate is to engage and educate those who have not done well in the Primary School Leaving Examination.

From 2008, we will see the end of the streaming into EM1, EM2 and EM3[4] bands and the introduction of a more "a la carte" menu selection of study to cater to varying levels of ability and perhaps, more importantly, address the issue of stigmatisation of children who struggle in schools. We must not destroy our children's sense of self-worth and self-esteem. This approach will hopefully also help to lower the attrition rate in schools. Our target is to halve the dropout rate at primary and secondary school levels from 3 percent to 1.5 percent by 2010.[5]

We also want to provide greater educational pathways to recognise different talent and widen the definition of success. For example, the Singapore Sports School started in 2004. Next year, the School of the Arts will open its doors for aspiring young

---

[4] EM1, EM2 and EM3 refer to English and Mother Tongue at each of three levels of ability.

[5] This target has been met. "The overall proportion of each Primary One (P1) cohort that does not complete secondary education has fallen from 4% in 2000 to less than 1% in the past 5 years." Quoted from *Parliamentary Replies*, Ministry of Education, http://www.moe.gov.sg/media/parliamentary-replies/2014/04/student-drop-out-rate-for-primary-secondary-and-ite-levels.php. Accessed 26 June 2015.

artists. We are also introducing greater flexibility in moving across the various streams and learning institutions — Institutes of Technical Education (ITEs), Polytechnics and Universities.

We are now seeing the results of our early investments in education. The percentage of Primary One students not completing secondary education has been steadily decreasing, from 4.3 percent in 2001 to 2.6 percent in 2005, with a corresponding increase in the rates of progression to post-secondary institutions. In the *Global Competitiveness Report 2005–2006* published by the World Economic Forum, Singapore's education system, as well as our science and mathematics education, was ranked first in terms of the ability to meet the needs of a competitive economy. Our educators stand at the crossroads of several intersecting strategic shifts in educational technology and orientation. If they can leverage on these resources and opportunities, we will celebrate many more successes in education. But more importantly, our children will gain immeasurably.

I believe that the next big frontier is pre-school education. The literature consistently suggests that early intervention through a high-quality pre-school education can help make up for deficiencies in home environments by way of ensuring school readiness. Yet 2006 figures show that 5 percent of children entering primary school have not attended pre-school. We want to ensure that as many children as possible are in pre-school, so that they get a good start in life.

Financial assistance schemes help ensure low-income children have access to pre-school education. The Kindergarten Financial Assistance Scheme (KiFAS), for example, provides a monthly fee subsidy for children to attend eligible kindergartens. A similar emphasis is placed on promoting access to high-quality childcare, which is likewise found to support the early development of children.

The common thread that runs through the childcare, pre-school and formal school systems is the passion and commitment of teachers. I salute you in your roles as trustees of our children's education and future. As Henry Adams once said, "A teacher affects eternity; he can never tell where his influence stops."[6]

Securing Safety

"My wish for children in Singapore is for all children to grow up in a safe environment with no wars, fighting, or killing. Everyone loves one another as one big family." — Wong Wen Kong, 9

This child's wish is a reminder that for some children, home is a battlefield filled with pain and sadness. Some families face problems like poverty, violence, substance abuse and other crises, which put the child's safety at risk. Under such circumstances, the government and the community have the responsibility to step in to deal with these family problems to ensure that the child's wellbeing is protected.

A key instrument for protecting children from abuse and neglect is the Children and Young Persons Act. The Act also provides for treatment of child abuse and neglect. The Child Protection Service (CPS) at MCYS (now the Ministry of Social and Family Development) is the key agency bearing statutory responsibility to protect children from abuse and neglect. CPS works in partnership with other agencies, such as the police, schools, hospitals and social service agencies, to ensure an integrated system of timely intervention for victims of child abuse or neglect.

The incidence of child abuse in Singapore is low. In the last five years, about 175 cases of child abuse were investigated each year. Whilst the number is small relative to the entire cohort of children in Singapore, we have a duty of care towards these children. Every case is a future robbed.

Prime Minister Lee Hsien Loong, in his speech at the opening of the Centre for Promoting Alternatives to Violence, or PAVE,

---

[6] Henry Adams, *The Education of Henry Adams* (Boston: Massachusetts Historical Society, 1907). Only 100 copies were privately published by the author but the text was reprinted and published in 1918 by the Massachusetts Historical Society. The quotation is from Chapter 20.

spoke of the key thrusts of our efforts against violence. I think these are worth reiterating today. The key thrusts are: strong legislation, practical policies and effective programmes that address both perpetrators and victims, and upstream measures such as public education aimed at strengthening families. These have served us well and remain central to our effort to make Singapore a safe place for children.

Our experience with child protection cases has been that ill-treatment sometimes begins as a caregiver's reaction to the child's behaviour. Poor understanding of the child's developmental needs, inability to cope with the child's challenging behaviour, and unrealistic expectations of the child, can all contribute to a weak parent–child relationship that could escalate to ill-treatment. Family crises could add to the stress. These realities mean a holistic intervention approach is needed to tackle child abuse.

The MCYS (now MSF) has, since 2004, also adopted the concept of permanency planning aimed at making informed and timely decisions on a child's long-term care. This planning process is initiated early in the supervision process, through interventions, assessments and discussions with professionals, parents, kin and significant others, and ensures that the responsibility for the care of a child does not switch from placement to placement indefinitely.

The work of protecting our children is physically and emotionally draining. I have heard countless stories of social workers and counsellors, Children's Society workers included, moved to tears at the sight of children who have been beaten, scalded or sexually abused. Difficult as it is, these workers carry on, sometimes being the difference between what makes or breaks the child. Society owes this dedicated group of individuals a great debt of gratitude. I thank you all for your service to our children and to Singapore.

Nurturing Families

"My wish for children in Singapore is for them to have a happy family! Whether rich or poor, everyone deserves a family to care

and love them. I wish for every child to have a happy home to return to." — Jeanine Cheok, 11

"My wish for children in Singapore is that they will grow up in a family full of love, trust, and care." — Geraldine Mok, 13

Families are central to the lives of children. Children need a supportive, loving environment to grow in, and role models to guide them into adulthood. Much evidence shows that where these factors are not present in the home, the child is at risk of failure.

Parents compete with other powerful sources of influence, including the internet, the media, and all the temptations of modern youth culture. As parents, we can deal with these influences in one of two ways: shield our children from them, or provide our children with strong foundations to help them make the right decisions. I believe in the latter. And the best way to do so is to reflect the right values through our own actions. As Robert Fulghum put it, "Don't worry that children never listen to you; worry that they are always watching you."[7]

---

[7] A well-known quote attributed without precise source. Robert Fulghum is an American author most famous for his book *All I Really Need to Know I Learned in Kindergarten* (New York: Ballantine Books, 1986).

However, effective parenting requires a deliberate effort, hence our heavy investment in parent education through the Parent Education in Pre-Schools (PEPS) and School Family Education (SFE) programmes. These offer a continuum of parenting and family life programmes, and cover issues such as parent–child relationships, parenting, marriage, financial planning and work–life harmony, from the pre-school to junior college level.

We recognise, of course, that some parents need more convincing than others on the importance of their role in their children's lives. Sometimes, the courts mandate counselling for parents whose children have been abused or whose children run afoul of the law. It is my fervent hope that more parents will embrace their role as key pillars of support and guidance for the next generation.

Embracing Diversity, Ensuring Inclusion

> *"My wish for children in Singapore is for people to respect each other's race. They will not make fun of each other. This will make them live in harmony." — Vivian Feng, 9*

> *"My wish for children in Singapore is to always be happy and healthy. I hope we will not be biased against each other just because another may be physically/mentally challenged; I hope we embrace each other's disabilities and look beyond that." — Yap Shi Kaye, 17*

As we develop as a city of possibilities, our children will explore and experience diverse pathways. This diversity is increasingly expressed in a manner that goes beyond race and culture. Nonetheless, an embrace of racial and cultural diversity remains crucial. A respect for and appreciation of racial and cultural diversity is not just a key ingredient for social harmony in Singapore, but a necessary one for an environment that is free from prejudice and stereotyping, and hence nurturing to children of all heritages. It is in this spirit that the government has, for example, encouraged and offered incentives for the pursuit of Chinese and Malay as third languages in schools. Language is a basic but powerful tool for our children to bridge differences.

Our concept of cultural diversity should also extend beyond our four major races. As more people from around the world sink their roots in Singapore, we must ensure an environment that welcomes them, particularly the children, with open arms. We must do all we can to ensure their integration into Singapore society so that we can, in turn, be enriched by the perspectives and experiences they bring with them.

Likewise, we can all do well to take heed from Shi Kaye's sanguine wish for everyone to "embrace each other's disabilities and look beyond that". How a society cares for the disabled reflects the kind of society it is. The Enabling Masterplan for 2007 to 2011, which has recently been announced, is a wide-ranging masterplan which looks into services for people with disabilities. More concretely, for school-going children, there will be more funding and support for Special Education (SPED), including cross posting of teachers from MOE's mainstream schools to SPED. A purpose-built SPED school is also on the cards to be completed by next year.

There will also be more Special Needs Officers and support for children with disabilities in mainstream schools. MOE has set aside some $50 million per year, to equip mainstream schools to better support students with special needs in their midst.

Children with disabilities particularly need support during their early years. To that end, we extended the Foreign Domestic Worker Levy Concession to families with disabled members, as well as starting a Caregivers Training Grant in October this year, to empower these families. More such initiatives will also be understudied by the Standing Committee on Disability which is chaired by my Permanent Secretary. Through the Committee, we hope to address disability issues holistically and maximise the potential of each and every person with a disability.

Securing Our Future — The Road Ahead

So where are we now and where do we want to be? What have we learnt from our experiences thus far? What should we do given the challenges before us? Allow me to share my thoughts on what I see as key strategies for the future.

Seeding an Agenda for Our Children

> "My wish for children in Singapore is that the potential of children of Singapore will be fully developed and used to build a better Singapore." — Chan Pei Hao, 11

Our children have told us that the key to securing their future resides in promoting health, providing quality education, securing their safety, embracing diversity and nurturing families. Our goal must be to achieve the best possible outcomes for children in all these areas. My challenge to all involved in the care of children is to embrace our shared responsibilities in pursuing a comprehensive agenda for our children.

Let me propose four basic principles to guide this agenda. First is the principle of child-centricity and a whole-child approach to policy and planning. We must be ready and committed to placing the child at the core of what we do, and ensure that all our policies and practices are framed by what is best for the child. We must be committed to addressing the child's needs in a holistic manner, going beyond seeing isolated issues of health, education and protection, for example.

Second, we must be committed to enhancing and integrating service delivery for all children. We want to ensure access, affordability, but most of all, quality of care in all our services. Of particular importance is how we recognise the interconnectedness of services and optimise these links to ensure that no needs are left unmet and no child falls through the cracks.

Third, the provision of specialised help, particularly to vulnerable and special groups, where necessary. It is inevitable that some children need more help than others due to their particular circumstances. In such cases, we must intervene early and effectively to avoid a lifetime of disadvantage.

And finally, a shared sense of responsibility amongst all agencies and individuals. We must believe that we have a responsibility towards our children and that collectively, we can and must safeguard their interests and wellbeing.

I would like to take this opportunity to commend the Singapore Children's Society for its efforts in protecting vulnerable children. It has been heartening to see how they have grown over the last 55 years. Indeed, the efforts of the Society are shining examples of shared ownership of our agenda for children in reaching out to and caring for our children, whether through their Tinkle Friend helpline, Project CABIN or student care and family care or other services.

Source: *The Straits Times* © Singapore Press Holdings Limited. Reprinted with permission.

Encouraging Participation

> *"My wish for children in Singapore is to get a chance to be listened to by adults and to be respected, and to get more attention." — Nicole Lee, 11.*

As we work towards creating a Singapore fit for children, we must also recognise the role that our children play in creating their destinies. Their participation would lend robustness and inspiration to the process. We must engage children as active partners in this process and not approach them as mere recipients of our policies. We must also be mindful of how national trends affect our children. We must work together to find ways to make their concerns more visible and mainstream in our mindset and across our institutions.

Conclusion: The Journey of Childhood

I have come to the conclusion that it is time to conduct a comprehensive review of the Children and Young Persons Act and all our programmes focussed on vulnerable children and dysfunctional families. We will consult our community partners and the general public.

Let me leave you with two final quotes from our children:

> *"My wish for children in Singapore is that every child can grow up to be a great person." — Bilal, 13*

> *"My wish for children in Singapore is to have a BOEING 747 and to travel around the world — plus a pilot in the plane."*
> *— Marcus Cheong, 9*

These are big dreams, but they embody the great hope that should characterise every childhood. So let us encourage our children to dream and to aspire. Their ability to dream and the destiny of Singapore are closely intertwined. The bigger their dreams, the greater a nation we will become.

CHAPTER TWO

Children and Childhood in the Singapore Chinese Family: Some Observations over Five Decades

Ann Wee

About the Speaker

Ann Wee has lived in Singapore since 1950, and is the doyenne of the social work profession here. Born in the North of England, she married the late Harry Wee, a Singapore lawyer. She had a war-time teaching qualification from London, but, she says, "I had really wanted to work in the Welfare Department." However, she started teaching at the Methodist Girls' School (MGS) because there was a shortage of teachers, and because the headmaster of the Anglo-Chinese School lived next door to her parents-in-law, and so there was "some pressure". But once started, she adds, "I had a truly happy time at MGS, and greatly valued the teacher and pupil friends that I made there." Nevertheless, after a few years of this, she managed to switch to social work, to which she devoted herself for the rest of her long and distinguished career. As she did so she accumulated a tremendous resource of experience, together with relevant skills such as a grasp of Cantonese. She has witnessed — and been actively involved in — the social transformations in an independent Singapore, both professionally and from the vantage point of an observer embedded in a local family.

We sometimes think psychologists study people, but the people who really study people are called anthropologists, and Ann Wee's academic grounding is indeed originally in that discipline. However, it is through her work in what was originally the colonial government Social Welfare Department, followed by the University of Malaya Social Studies Department, and finally the Department of Social Work, NUS, that she has put her mark on Singapore. She has been decorated for her public service and achievement, with the Public Service Star (BBM) in 1974, and BBM bar in 2004. She is still a Visiting Associate Professorial Fellow at NUS, after 32 years as a hugely successful and respected Head, and the great majority of Singapore social workers alive today have passed through her hands. Speaking to them, one soon realises the high esteem in which she is held.

To have a conversation with Ann Wee is to enter a goldmine of oral history. The book committee listened entranced to stories and recollections of times when some of them were not even born. She remembers the Singapore Children's Society starting in the backyard of a Victoria Street crèche, in 1952. Social work was not professionalised at that time, with established procedures not yet in place, nor was it knowledge-based. Professor Wee has sat on committees of the Children's Society, and has been a true friend and supporter. She has also sat for decades on the Panel of Advisors to the Juvenile Court and this experience profoundly informs her perspective on Singapore children and families.

She is keenly aware of differences across culture and over time. In times past, when large families were the norm and children were an insurance for support in old age, she remembers mothers lying about their "tiger" daughters' age to get them married. Such girls[1] were also particularly difficult to get adopted, and were often abandoned. Occasionally, too, it was difficult to place baby boys for adoption. Stricter criteria were applied to boys, as they would take the family name. Girls, on the other hand, were only temporary members of the family. The government, of course, was originally concerned to get the

---

[1] Born in the Chinese Zodiac Year of the Tiger.

birth rate down, and success in this resulted in children being much more valued and invested in today than in previous decades. One could even say that in Singapore, in earlier times, adoption was the family planning of the poor. Later, it became clear, says Professor Wee, that the government overshot the target when it came to family planning. It may have underestimated the impact of a rise in income, plus limited HDB apartment space and widespread contraception, on how families planned their children.

Ann Wee married into a Chinese family and thus experienced first-hand the differences between English and Chinese expectations of family life, though she also feels her parents-in-law did not themselves have a typical upbringing. Her father-in-law was the adopted son of a *Kapitan China* from Indonesia (at that time, the Dutch East Indies). He was sent to St Joseph's Institution aged nine, and, later, to Aberdeen Grammar School in Scotland, while still wearing his hair in a queue. He came to Singapore in 1919 and volunteered at St Andrew's Hospital, where he met his wife. This wife, Ann Wee's future mother-in-law, was born in Hong Kong and schooled in London.

The newly-wed Ann Wee soon noticed the many differences, some subtle, that distinguished English from Chinese families in Singapore. For example, unlike in England, where young people waited until they were spoken to, in her new family, courtesy required the young to address the older folk first. The English would never give cash to social equals, only to children or social inferiors; but the Chinese give cash at funerals. The Chinese were also blunt when it came to family dealings — the outsiders' view of elaborate courtesies only reflected what outsiders or the public saw. If Ann Wee's mother-in-law did not agree with a dress that she had bought, she'd say straight out, "*Aiyah*, what did you buy that for? It doesn't suit you!" Her mother-in-law also gave her good advice, including advice not to learn *mah-jong*, so that she would not have to spend hours in chit-chat with mother-in-law's friends.

Now that families have got smaller, they still remain close, but Professor Wee worries about the single old. In extended families, old

Ann Wee at 18 years

people with no children of their own were looked after by nieces or nephews. And after the war, there were many single women, because a lot of men died in the war. So, many older singles, especially women, formed partnerships with each other, to avoid loneliness in old age. These civic partnerships were not to do with sex. They were a form of practical mutual support. Nowadays, we think of civic same-sex partnerships as an alternative to marriage, but Professor Wee would revive the idea of legal but platonic partnerships or relationships for single people, say over 45, as a form of social protection, companionship and housing provision for the future elderly with no families to fall back on.

Professor Wee's lecture is about children and childhood in the Singapore Chinese family. This reflects its personal nature. Ann Wee modestly felt she lacked the personal experience to comment extensively on children and childhood in minority groups. But no one reading the chapter that has resulted from her talk could fail to see the universal nature of many of her observations, and their relevance to Singaporeans of all races.

The 2nd Lecture, delivered 15 November 2008

In the late 1950s, two little Singapore Chinese sisters were bathed, suppered, and into their pyjamas, by the time their father came home late from the family business. At the sound of his car in the driveway, they trotted to meet him. And over a long period during their childhood, a much-enjoyed (and nostalgically recalled) nightly choral ritual ensued (in Hokkien); father slumped in a lounge chair, with an arm around each snuggling daughter.

"Why is papa late?" he asked, opening the chorale
"Papa is late because he works very hard"
"Why does papa work very hard?"
"Papa works very hard to earn money"
"Why does papa need to earn money?"
"So that we can have a good life"
"Why does papa want you to have a good life?"
"Because papa loves us" (an exchange of hugs)
"And when you grow up?"
"We will cook papa a nice tasty dish of pork"
(General dissolving into hugs and giggles, and then off to bed)

By the norms of the 1950s "papa" was a modern father, demonstratively affectionate towards his children when they were young, and ensuring his daughters had the same educational opportunities as their brothers, when the time came. But still, there was the theme of parental love involving sacrifice; sacrifice which will be repaid by the children later on.

In this particular family the lesson was instilled in a teasing, affectionate manner, but frequently it was articulated in much more blunt terms. Indeed children learned early, and in no uncertain terms, that they were indebted to their parents, who suffered hardship and made sacrifices in order to bring them up. Because of this the children incurred a lifelong responsibility to repay this debt.

In societies where there are no government-regulated and/or other organised systems of preparing for old age, children have always been, and still are, virtually the only social insurance system around. But perhaps because of the "afterlife component", the Chinese family "blue-print" included an unusually articulate recognition of this fact, to ensure that the lesson was learned well and learned young. The parents' wellbeing, not only during their old age in this world, but also post mortem in the next, depended on filial male descendants: the destiny of becoming a homeless ghost in the Chinese afterlife was too horrible to contemplate.

An early observation, soon after my 1950 arrival in Singapore, also threw some light on this theme of child training. This related to the manner in which mothers and children crossed streets together. I recalled in my own childhood, negotiating the hazards of road crossing, mutually clasping hands with my mother. I had hitherto neither witnessed nor dreamed of any other possible method. But the Singapore mother, in contrast, grasped her child's wrist, in a manner which left the little hand dangling and passive. "Yes," said my Singapore friends, when I commented on this, "that way is much safer." Really? Was this degree of safety truly needed, I pondered. I did not recall that the hand-clasp method, to which I had been

The New Paper © Singapore Press Holdings Limited. Reprinted with permission

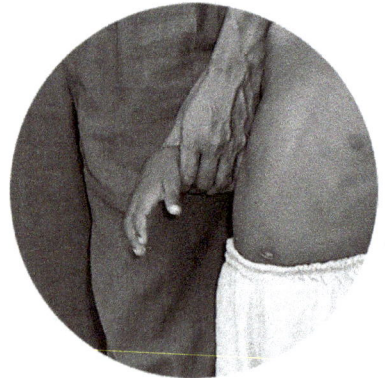

The Straits Times © Singapore Press Holdings Limited. Reprinted with permission.

accustomed, had resulted in a high rate of child mortality on the roads. Clearly the difference related to something more than preservation of child life.

I recollected this difference in road-crossing technique when I came to have small children of my own, and was warned, not once but on numerous occasions, not to "chit-chat" with my pre-schoolers, or they would (and I quote) "take advantage" and "not respect you". For these friends and acquaintances, parenting was perhaps not a training in reciprocity, but a control, "top-down" activity, in which the establishment of a healthy respectful attitude on the part of the children towards their elders was a priority element in the parenting "mission statement". Those passive dangling little hands fitted into this picture.

Another early culture-learning experience on family came through my being required to conduct a school oral English examination for girls aged 13 or 14. In the interest of standardisation I was provided with a list of questions with which to initiate this mutual ordeal. "How many brothers and sisters do you have?" If the answer was, for example, "six", I, the newly arrived western-reared examiner, not unnaturally envisaged a brood of seven children. But this was cross-cultural ignorance. My young victim did not see herself as an individual with a number of siblings, but as a member of a group of six. The focus was on the group, not on herself. A subtle but very real distinction, and an introduction to the structured and corporate character of the Chinese family.

This learning was reinforced as I came to work for four years in the same school, and enjoyed close friendship with the staff room crowd. In coffee break conversations my colleagues made frequent reference to their brothers and sisters. Yet never once, over the whole four years, did I learn the personal name of even one of their siblings. It was always "my second brother", or "my third sister". These relationships were often warm and close, but clearly siblings were seen as members of a structure rather than as named individuals.

Some scholars have likened the historic Chinese family blue-print/model to a corporation, where the parent "CEOs" were training the sons for future managerial roles. Or, in the case of girls, the parents were preparing them for subordinate roles in

For most of us in Singapore, it's still the father who calls the shots, and the children are not viewed as individuals but part of a family. Now, as a parent myself, I would like to seek your advice on how to change this mindset.

Well, I think one of the problems of past generations was that children didn't get the feeling that anybody listened to them. Listening doesn't mean you have to agree. Parents need confidence that they do have some standards to set. But let's not be fussy about everything; let's decide on a few things that are absolutely cast-iron and be relaxed whenever we can.

However, I do think that children greatly value the feeling that they are listened to. Little tiny children, who are probably very boring to listen to, are at an age when you click with them. If you listen to them when they're young and boring, then they go on talking to you when they're teenagers. But if you don't listen to them when they're small, they're not interested in talking to you when they're teenagers; they've got other people to talk to. So one of the few things I'm really comfortable at saying is that in establishing this listening and being prepared for years of boring chit-chat, you clinch and bond the relationship. You don't have to agree with them, but be prepared to discuss with them.

Be expressive. And if you lose your temper with them, say, *you know you really provoked mummy. She didn't really want to lose her temper, but when you do a thing like that, mummy's human; she gets angry.* So the children understand the kind of texture of the relationship, and the problems of being a parent. I think being there for them is terribly important, but I don't think children are comfortable without a framework. I think children long for some kind of framework, and if they're testing, they're testing where the boundaries are.

— From the Question & Answer session

another corporate group — a group not of the girls' own choosing. Family corporate advantage, not individual feelings, would be the basis on which the match would be made. This model fits a top-down parent–child relationship, cautious in demonstrative affection or in the familiarity of chit-chat, which could interfere with the development of a healthy respect for their elders (the family managers) on the part of the young, who were in one sense the apprentices in training.

This model also helps to explain the generally observed low level of emotional involvement with daughters in historic China. In her early teens, tradition decreed the daughter must be sent as a bride to another family corporation, usually at some great distance away. Thereafter her natal family would be unable to help her in any way, even if she received harsh treatment in her new home. In these circumstances, deep emotional commitment to a beloved child you were helpless to defend would have been a recipe for endless parental misery, indeed for depressive mental ill-health. In the words of one scholar, the Chinese family gave up access to daughters' wellbeing, in exchange for full control of daughters-in-law and wives.

Far-away marriages were never usual in the South Seas, but it took some generations for a change in attitudes to daughters. In that same girls' school to which I have referred, I recall the feisty principal (the great Mrs Handy of cookery book fame) having furious arguments at the threshold of her office, in Malay, with Peranakan mothers. Mrs Handy was always trying to dissuade these mothers from taking their daughters out of school before completing secondary education. The usual argument, on the part of the mothers (repeated on numerous occasions), was that by her early 20s the girl would marry, and "those other people" (I quote) would reap the benefits from money spent on schooling by her own parents. Family priorities, not individual development of one member, must come first. Even then, and in Singapore and among the Straits Chinese, daughters were still to some extent "goods on which you lose". They were yours only temporarily,

Is filial piety a necessary value in modern society? Western societies seem to manage without it.

Well, I think underlying filial piety is filial love. And I think the piety gets kind of moved over to love. Now remember, I was first here at a time when families were very different. But let me tell you, if I had been chatting with my young teenage friends in England, and my mother had come in to the room, she would have been very hurt if we had not included her in the conversation.

I was so surprised when I first came to Singapore that if I was going out with my young Chinese friends and we visited their family home, if the old people came into the room, we stopped talking. It wasn't respectful to go on talking and that was because you showed respect by distance. And I think, as I've said, that gradually as family life is becoming more informal, underlying piety is love even if people don't express it that way. They say, *I cared for my parents in the old-fashioned days of course, by making offerings.* Terry Tan in his recent book[2] recalls his father's wake, in which ceremonially they fed the corpse saying *Father, you looked after us; we want to see you go to the next world with good food.* Now maybe that's piety, but underneath it is a message of loving, even though it's expressed in a formal way. And I think that this is a better transition where, in a sense, grown-up children become the home-grown pals, if you like, of the parents, but still giving the parents some dignity. So I think if we look at what's underlying piety, it is caring and loving in this very formal way. And gradually this becomes transferred into a loving and a more informal relationship where you show caring by including your parents in your activities, not by respectfully keeping at a distance.

— *From the Question & Answer session*

---

[2]   Terry Tan, *Stir-Fried and not Shaken* (Singapore: Monsoon Books, 2008).

until they fulfilled their destiny as members of their husbands' families.

And only as a mother in her husband's family was a woman assured of filial care in this world and the next. Once married, she and her children had no part in the ancestor worship of her natal family. Only as a mother of sons was her own wellbeing in old age and in the Chinese afterlife assured: only her sons and her sons' children could look after her when she became old, and tend to the needs of her soul after she passed away.

This distinction was brought home to me when I worked in the Social Welfare Department, in 1955–1956. I was asked to interview an elderly Peranakan Chinese lady who had appealed to her married son's multinational employer to transfer him back from Kuala Lumpur to Singapore, on the grounds that she missed her grandchildren. In the course of our conversation it arose that in Singapore she was close to five married daughters, all of whom had children who visited her often. "But *Bebe*," I explained (using the address form correct for this lady's age), "with all those grandchildren around, it will be difficult for your son's employer to accept that you are lonely." The reply came at me like a cannon ball: "Those are not mine! Those are other people's grandchildren!" The look of utter bewilderment on the lady's face (that I should have failed to see this from the outset) was a cross-cultural learning experience most profound!

Confucian restraint in physical demonstrations of love and affection in family life has often been interpreted by casual western observers as a sign of coldness in family relationships. Their own growing-up experience has made it difficult for these westerners to envisage any ways of expressing love, other than in the articulate and hugging, body-contact model with which they are familiar. Adherence to this model in seeking to understand Chinese family life can mean the missing of indicators of caring and warmth well understood within Chinese culture.

My dear (and alas long gone) friend Dr Chin Ai Li described coming home from morning school in the 1920s, and announcing to her father that she was top of her class. "Humph," he said, and went on reading his newspaper. But at the lunch table he announced casually that the family would be eating at a restaurant that evening. Nothing further was said, but round the table, mother and children exchanged sly smiling glances, which father ignored. Even in old age Ai Li recalled a physical sensation of warmth and joy, and a sense of being valued, praised and cared for: no less real for the roundabout way in which she had received from her father, the message of parental love and approval.

Before Ai Li recalled this incident in her own life, I had described to her my own 1950 visit to the wards of St Andrew's Mission Children's Hospital, which was situated in one of the poorest slum districts in Singapore's Chinatown. The visiting hour arrived, and in trooped the mothers (many looking worn and shabbily attired, as I recall), each carrying a small tiffin carrier of cooked food. To the amazement of my culturally ignorant eyes, not one mother kissed or hugged her child. She felt the child's forehead, perhaps squeezed the upper arm, but pretty promptly sat down on the bedside stool and began coaxingly to feed her sick child with chicken, either as porridge, or prepared in some other way.

This was long before the introduction of factory-style poultry rearing, and chicken was still very much a luxury food, appearing on poor tables only at Chinese New Year, if at all. So the message conveyed to the child was very clear: "My mother has spared cash to buy and cook a chicken for me. Wow, I am really important to her, and she really cares for me!"

Food as the language of love emerges as a recurring theme, and indeed keeps popping up and is with us still. Not long ago a Probation Officer was striving to improve relations between a sulky teenager and a caring but inarticulate father. Discovering that father and son watched TV football together (in cold silence!), the PO suggested the father buy some snacks for his son. The PO related to me how the usually sullen boy came beaming to his next reporting session. "My Dad bought me a packet of crisps!" Love in action!

In the 1960s, I had reason to set an essay requiring students to continue the following introductory sentence: "That was the day I knew my parents loved me…" Repeatedly, up came the illness and/or chicken theme, so often that it seemed amazing that this had not produced in these English-schooled young people from conservative Chinese homes a universal condition of hypochondria, seeking neurotic re-enactments of the warmly recalled childhood experience. Perhaps they were saved from this fate by some intrinsic integration into a culture where, even in complicating modernity, the rules of the "family game" were still understood.

Even when one has read and learned about the Confucian group orientation in family life, individual examples come as something of a surprise when first encountered on the hoof. In the late 1960s Chinese and English education was still provided in totally separate school systems. A fresh graduate from the then Chinese medium Nanyang University, now Dr Lee Chong Kau, came to attend social work training at the then University of Singapore. He chose as his research topic an open-ended study of factors which led families (quite a large sample involving four schools) to choose either Chinese or English education for their children. Both he and myself as his supervisor anticipated that parental choices would be on an "either/or" basis. We thought we would find out the reasons why the children of a particular family were enrolled in one or the other system. Was it because parents felt that one system was superior to the other?

In many families we found a much more complex situation, in which one stream was felt to be far superior, but where the needs of the family as a group required that one child should be sent to the other stream. "Chinese education is much the best, but we need someone in the family to cope with government letters." Or, "Nowadays English education leads to better prospects, but we need one family member who can keep up the correspondence with the relatives in China."

The analysis did not allow for identifying any gender or birth order bias in the choice of sacrificial lamb selected for the "less good" school experience. Nor did we encounter any embarrassment that the family was deliberately depriving one child of what they themselves regarded as the best education. The parental responsibility was to do what was best for the family as a whole. The family, not the individual member, must always come first.

Indeed the family must survive, even if individual members do not. In the late 1970s, many Confucian Vietnamese took to small boats, desperate to escape from what they found to be an intolerable politico-economic system. Commonly mother and some children would travel in one boat, father and other children in another. The risks of not surviving the sea journey were lamentably high, and the basis of planning was that by separating into two groups, the chances of one family "remnant" making it to safety were thereby increased.

The priority was that the family must survive, even though some members were lost. This was very different from the "live or die we all go together" attitude, which I personally recalled in wartime Britain, when issues of evacuation from high-risk bombed areas were discussed. One culture saw only a priority of relationships; the other had a perception of family as an institution of greater significance than any of the individual members.

Perhaps it was this emphasis on family wellbeing as a priority over individual relationships, which influenced the Chinese attitude to childhood as a life stage. A very perceptive woman doctor, volunteering service in family planning clinics in the late 1950s, noted a difference between her Chinese and Malay women patients. This was well before the fertility-limiting "stop at two" policy: the goal in those days of very large families was maternal and child health, and a well-spaced family, preferably limited to four children.

The doctor commented that her Malay patients wanted to have their babies well-spaced, so, as she put it, "the cradle would never be empty". On the other hand, the ideal for her Chinese patients was "one, two, three, four and then 'cut'" — the collo-quial term for sterilisation. Child rearing was a burden, and the quicker you got through it the better. She used to laugh that her Chinese patients would have loved her dearly, if she could have taught them how to give birth to young adults instead of babies.

Comparable observations were made by a perceptive young Singaporean, Miss Sally Tan, who around 1960 spent one year at a college in the United States. She pondered on the attitude of the mothers of her college-age American friends, compared to the mother–teen relations of her own growing-up experience in Singapore. These American mothers seemed loath to see their daughters entering the thresholds of adulthood, and would reminisce endlessly and nostalgically about their daughters' baby and childhood days. This theme was so persistent that Sally sensed that the mothers regretfully watched their daughters growing up and experienced this as somehow symbolising their own loss of youth.

Miss Tan was much puzzled by this, being accustomed to a culture in Singapore where, at that time, growing old was almost welcomed, as the period when one received the due respect earned from a well-spent life. Indeed in their reports, Census Directors had regularly bewailed the tendency of the Singapore population to lie, claiming to be older than their true age. Quite the reverse of the problem of Census takers in western countries, where respondents tended to claim to be younger than was truly the case.

As part of her social work training in Singapore, Miss Tan therefore undertook a study of the relationship between teenage girls and their mothers in her own society. She did indeed find Singapore mothers welcoming their daughters' newly burgeoning adult status. Where American mothers had claimed their daughters were becoming hard to relate to, the Singapore mothers saw their girls entering an age of reason and increased capacity for taking some family responsibility, thereby reducing some of their own burdens and cares.

Miss Tan found that mothers saw the end of childhood as the point where they felt they could no longer send their daughters on errands. As her supervisor I found this puzzling, and inconsistent with the subordinate role of even adult children, in the "blueprint" Chinese family. I had assumed that even as young adults, Chinese family members would be at the beck and call of their elders. I commented on this, and on the cultural contrast, that when I visited my own mother in England (I was then aged about 40), she would have no hesitation about sending me on errands. She would say something like, "Be a pal, run upstairs, and get my glasses." "Ah," responded the observant Miss Tan, "but there is no way in Chinese in which a mother could say 'be a pal'. She could either give an order, and you wouldn't order an adult child. Or she could say 'please' and for a Chinese mother that would be unthinkable."

Miss Tan's study tended to confirm the impression that childhood was about rearing adults, and was not a phenomenon to be valued for its own sake. It also gave hints of some formality in the relationship between parents and adult children, and provided interesting insights into the way in which language could set limits to the range of options in parent–child interaction.

On Language Policy and Intergenerational Communication

I find in Singapore that the English spoken doesn't have a great many sayings in it, whereas the English that I grew up with is full of metaphors and similes. You would say *that's not cricket*, which is obviously, you know, nothing to do with cricket. I don't find Singapore's English to be full of these sayings, and friends tell me that Mandarin is also a functional goal-oriented language, whereas dialect is full of them. I mean, if you're a teacher and you're speaking Cantonese, and it's hard to get the message across to your student, you'd say *it's like trying to drag a cow up a tree*, you know? I understand that Teochew dialect is also full of sayings.

There was a time when the grandparents didn't speak English. Then, children often spoke the home dialect of their grandparents. Obviously Mandarin education has brought tremendous benefits. But what worries me a little is that family values came through in the dialect. I don't know whether we have managed to engineer it so that they come through in the local Mandarin. I'm really quoting from elderly Chinese-educated friends, who have been concerned because it was granny's proverbs and sayings that taught you your values. I'm not against Mandarin; it's for progress that we had to standardise and obviously our relationship with China is very important. But I think there have been costs that perhaps we didn't or couldn't strategise for. I don't know.

I think the Malay community does not have this problem because I think the Malay family still interacts very comfortably even if they're English-educated. Although Malay friends tell me that it's very easy to tell the difference between someone who is thinking in English before speaking in Malay and somebody who is thinking and speaking in Malay.

So language positively, inevitably, makes a difference, and not just in this country. There have been language policy moves in education in English which have had tremendous impact on the way English is used. I heard of somebody who was turned down for a BBC job because her English was too good; they wanted somebody with the flavour of a locality. Now that is a complete change. Having a language policy is a very common political tool and it always produces some pros and cons.

— From the Question & Answer session

This also helped to explain my own 1940s experience at London University, where my Singapore Chinese friends could not understand how family custom of those days required that I write home to my parents (in the North of England) at least once a week (long distance phone calls were not then an option). What could I possibly have to say every week? When I gave examples of the trivia with which these letters home were filled, my Singapore friends were quite shocked — in Chinese you could only write to parents about major matters, such as college requirements, changes of residence, or finance. Not only were trivial things, like social outings or problems with the hot water system, unsuitable for a letter home, my friends could not envisage how such matters could be expressed in the written word.

As the Singapore family changes under the impact of economic and other influences, it seems that cultural differences between East and West become somewhat reduced. In each society the family continues to have a certain distinct cultural "flavour", but differences are no longer so extreme.

The little girls in my initial anecdote are now in their fifties, and they and their siblings have indeed, metaphorically, cooked the "nice dish of tasty pork" for their parents, which they promised "papa" so long ago. Economic developments have taken some family members overseas, but those still around, while not living under the same roof, keep in constant touch, and provide the care and arrangement-making assistance now needed by their parents. In fact, what they are providing is very much the caring, case-management role which is still a recognised feature of adult child/elderly parent relationships in the developed West.

Young Singapore parents can often be heard expressing the view that they do not expect support from their children when they themselves grow old, but they experience great anxiety in the fulfilment of their vision of the parental role. They probably have one, two, or three children, but they commonly spend on this small brood all they can afford in the way of aids to success and enrichment: tuition classes, tennis, ballet, music lessons and vacation camps; the lot. Indeed contemporary Singapore childhood has been likened to a pressure-cooker experience.

If you were a child in this age, in this time, how would you live your life? Do you have any advice for children?

Well, I'm afraid I can only think of it from the point of view of young parents, and I think one hopes that young parents will not over-pressure their children and that they will be able to think of their family life in terms of the family, rather than in competing with other people, so that they teach the children to compete with themselves and improve in that way. And that also they will be very careful to distinguish their love for the child from caring about their child's achievements. Children must be loved even if they don't achieve. And of course we always train probation officers to think: *you're not condemning the child; you're condemning the behaviour. That behaviour is stupid. You know how to do better. Not that you are stupid.* Otherwise you're pushing the child down. So it's very important that parents, even if they do give their child all these opportunities, don't convey the feeling that the child is only loved in terms of how well he or she achieves. I think perhaps that would be the only thing that I feel very safe saying that is absolutely essential for a child to feel, *I can do my best but if I don't get there, my parents will still care for me.* I think children really need that security. I don't know if I quite answered to your question but I can only get into the shoes of the parent. I find it too difficult to get totally into the shoes of the child.

— From the Question & Answer session

In the (Singapore) *Sunday Times* of 25 June 2006, a Chinese mother roughly the same age as "papa's" daughters expressed her philosophy of parenthood. "My greatest joy has been raising my children," she said. "I used to ask myself every night what I had done for them physically, culturally, spiritually, religiously and socially." She added that it was because of them that she had always worked very hard. Her final advice was, "The best thing you can do for your children is get out of their hair. You need to give them space to grow." "Papa" was Chinese-educated, but this mother is one full generation younger and English-educated through upper tertiary level; two very different views of preparing children for adult roles.

Cartoon by Yong Teck Meng

Metaphors have limited use, and cannot be carried too far, but as far as they go, they may help us to visualise reality. The "blue-print" Confucian family could be likened to a ship. The family members are the current crew, and for safety in rough seas and for efficient performance, the officers need to run a tight ship. Discipline is emphasised, and a respectful distance between officers and ratings is maintained. In-service training for the crew, and their shore-based training, is planned in terms of the ship's needs and the apprentice crew's preparation for future officer roles and responsibilities. At various ports of call, well-prepared young women members disembark and join other ships. And similarly, young women from elsewhere join this ship — already well-trained in their natal ship on shipboard rules.

Everyone is aware that at some point the young officers-in-training will take over the running of the ship. The personnel will change, but the ship will continue, each shift of crew having the maintenance (and if possible also the upgrading) of the ship as their main priority and responsibility.

In a similar vein, perhaps the western family more resembles an establishment under NASA, the United States National Aeronautics and Space Administration. According to its website, NASA is (and I quote) "dedicated to professional development, and to inspiring the next generation of astronauts". Their products are being trained for launch into space, not for roles in the ground establishment. Similarly, the western family is training its young, not for roles in the natal family base, but for final take-off, to be launched out into the world. The western family's satisfactions come from reflected glory, from pride in the galactic economic and social distances reached by the next generation. Nonetheless, as in the case of NASA, the family's "astronauts" are welcomed with rejoicing, whenever they make it safely back to base.

Indeed the family is also still the place to which you can return, even when mission is not accomplished.

Confucian and western families do start from different basic premises, as the exigencies of their historic political, economic and social contexts have prescribed. Upbringing in each system has ensured survival, and has proved to have in-built mechanisms for coping with change — and even with disaster and crisis management.

Do you have any advice to parents handling rebellious teenagers?

I think it's a time for making contracts. For example, I said to one of my granddaughters, *I don't mind how many holes you put in your ears and I don't mind if you put a hole in your nose because we know from centuries that these don't give people any adverse problems. But I absolutely would be upset if you put a stud in your tongue or your lips because we don't know if this might increase the chances of mouth cancer later on.* So I think you decide what is absolutely necessary to insist on but don't worry too much if they come home with pink hair. It's not going to do anybody any harm. The contract is, for instance, no argument about not having tattoos. They can paint their bodies purple but no question of tattoos, because those are often life-changing. Schools don't want you back until you've got rid of them and they cost $1,500 or something to excise even a small area.

You think, *what are the things that irritate me because it's not my style?* and *what are the things that really matter?* and you make contracts with the teenagers. That's the only suggestion I can make.

— From the Question & Answer session

But rapid change has rarely been experienced as an on-going and accepted way of life as it is today. Services to help build strengths and resilience in children have never been more needed. And helping children to cope in an age of change means helping children in their family setting, for we can only truly meet needs if we work systemically.

Side by side with service, the study of how families of all cultures cope with this world situation must be another priority — in the interests not only of children, but of us all.

CHAPTER THREE

Changing Social Mores: Protecting Children from Themselves?

Walter Woon

About the Speaker

Professor Walter Woon, former Attorney-General, former Nominated MP, has an exceptional list of achievements in his chosen profession, the Law. He is of Baba descent, and might be thought to have displayed early promise as a law-enforcer, being head prefect at Pasir Panjang Primary School and then a prefect at Raffles Institution. With a scholarship from DBS Bank to study law, he obtained his Bachelor of Laws (LL.B.) from the National University of Singapore, graduating in 1981 with first class honours. That same year, he also topped the postgraduate practice law course, winning the Aw Boon Haw and Aw Boon Par Memorial Prize. In 1983 he took a Master of Laws (LL.M.) degree with first class honours from St John's College, Cambridge, which he completed on a Commonwealth Academic Staff scholarship.

Professor Woon was called to the Singapore Bar in 1985. In 1988 he became a Sub-Dean of the NUS Faculty of Law, then served as Vice-Dean from 1991 to 1995. In 1999 he was appointed a Professor of Law. He was a Nominated Member of Parliament for three terms, from 1992 to 1996, and moved the private member's bill that became the Maintenance of Parents Act of 1995; it was the first law from a private member's bill since Singapore's independence and the only one by a

Nominated MP. In its issue of 5 December 1994, *Time* magazine picked Walter Woon as one of 100 young world leaders, the only Singaporean to make the list.

From 1995 to 1997, Professor Woon was Legal Adviser to the President of Singapore and the Council of Presidential Advisors. From 1997 to 2006, he was with the Foreign Service as Ambassador to Germany, then Belgium, and with accreditation to Greece, the European Union, the Netherlands, Luxembourg and the Vatican. In 2006, the Vatican made him a Knight Grand Cross of the Order of St. Gregory the Great.

After this tour of diplomatic duty, Professor Woon was appointed Second Solicitor-General in 2006, and Solicitor-General in 2007, when he was also made a Senior Counsel. He became Attorney-General in April 2008 and served for two years. It was while he was Attorney-General that he delivered the 3rd Singapore Children's Society Lecture. In the same year, he was also appointed a director of the Monetary Authority of Singapore and a member of the Presidential Council for Minority Rights. Professor Woon returned to the Law Faculty of NUS in 2010, and also became the first Dean of the Singapore Institute of Legal Education. He is currently Chairman of the Singapore International Law Society, and President of the Goethe Institute Singapore. Less well known is his proclivity for writing fiction as a form of relaxation, and he has four published novels.

As with several other speakers in this volume, reflecting recently on the Children's Society lecture led him to reiterate the concerns about values earlier expressed in the lecture. In the past, Professor Woon has publicly expressed some irritation with those in western societies who used the concept of human rights to criticise Singapore, which he sees as a matter where Singaporeans should determine their own lines of demarcation on what is or is not acceptable. Speaking with the book committee members, he revisited a similar kind of concern. He saw clearly that more needed to be done to combat early sexualisation of children in American and UK society, shown by phenomena such as beauty pageants for really young children and sexualised clothes for pre-adolescent children. He also felt that there had been an accompanying trend to treat sex as recreational, with casual or consensual sex mainstreamed. It was then hardly surprising that the problem of underage sex has not gone away.

The problem was, he felt, very much a matter of societal mores and values, including religious values. It depended critically, in his view, on parents' relationship with their children, and on their own example as role models, sometimes in the face of very different messages from peer groups. He felt it was troubling to see consenting children fall foul of the law, and ineffective to send teenagers to jail for sexual activity, especially when they did not feel they had done anything wrong. However, decriminalising underage sex, even by consenting partners, was not an answer either. Nor did he think that we could isolate ourselves from global trends.

He felt adolescents should be talking among themselves about their attitudes, but moderated by adults such as teachers or Children's Society staff who are not squeamish. Parents, felt Professor Woon, himself a parent, are squeamish about broaching such topics. They would tell youngsters about the "mechanics" but the "software", the feelings behind sex, they are not so willing to discuss. So, it might fall to others to draw them out and have a frank talk about what premarital sex actually means. He would, he said, suggest holding such sessions separately for males and females, as the dynamics would change if both sexes are put together. In the end, it comes down to which set of values will prevail, and which role models will be followed.

Walter Woon in the uniform of a Wolf Cub

The 3rd Lecture, delivered 31 October 2009

In the last few years we have seen a loosening of inhibitions, a change in attitude, when it comes to sexuality, especially sexuality in children; liberalisation is probably not quite the right word. The law, unfortunately, is still stuck in 19th- and 20th-century modes, and there are certain assumptions built into the law. It is these which this lecture is about.

Unfortunately, there is a little problem. When I was an academic, I had total freedom of speech, to say anything I like. But the further up the hierarchy you go, the smaller the area you can actually say anything about. So now, I am inhibited. And before I go on, I need to clarify some misconceptions in Singapore about the position of the Attorney-General. In most countries, the Attorney-General is a politician, is a member of the cabinet, a minister. He faces re-election. He has pressures from constituencies, pressures from the electorate.

This is not the case in Singapore. As Attorney-General, I don't have to stand for election. I am not a member of the ruling party and I am definitely not a politician. But this also means that I am not responsible for policy. People often send me letters saying, "please do this, please do that", but I have to say, "Thank you very much. I'd like to but I can't." In Singapore, policy is made by the Cabinet. The Cabinet and the Minister of Law are the ones who tell us, the Attorney-General's Chambers, what the policy is. Our job is to take instructions from the Government, and translate them into legal language. The policy is set by the ministry; we are merely the drafters.

That doesn't mean we cannot make suggestions, but ultimately, when it comes to what the law of Singapore is going to be, the decision is not made by the Attorney-General's Chambers. However, where we do have autonomy is in prosecution. The Attorney-General is the person who is in charge of prosecution. He is independent, in deciding who to prosecute, and who not to prosecute. So I don't tell the Minister about how to make the law and he doesn't tell me who to prosecute. But this then puts on us, the prosecution branch, quite a heavy burden, because we have to make a decision. We don't prosecute everybody who breaks the law, because if we did, the courts would be full of jay-walkers and litterbugs. There has to be some common sense, some priorities.

It is when we come to the prosecution of sexual offences that we have the most intractable problems, because different people have different ideas as to whether it is in the public interest to actually drag someone to court. It is a perfectly honest disagree-ment, it has to do with the sense of values that one has. It is noth-ing to do with liberalism, conservatism or libertinism; nothing to do with that. People do have these differences, and in the AG's Chambers, we also have differences when it comes to prosecu-tion. I will deal with this when I talk about the problems of pro-tecting children because of the way the law is structured.

The concept of childhood is actually relatively recent. I think it's probably 19th century because before that, the idea that children were something special, something other than small adults, was foreign to most cultures.[1] And I should define what I mean by children. I'm going to be using the word "children" in a very general sense. Legally of course, we make distinctions between children below the age of 13, below the age of 14, below the age of 16, below the age of 18, below 21 in various contexts. I will advert to that, rather than define the terms. I'm just going to use the word "children" as a generic term for people under 18. At common law, the age of majority is 21. So technically, if you are under 21, and I see many people here who look like they might be, you are an infant.

---

[1] This point is further elaborated by Professor Aline Wong in Chapter 4.

I understand there is agreement that you're not mature enough to be totally responsible for criminal activity as long as you're a child. But you may have a record of juvenile offences and these may become a criminal record. Is this something you can elaborate on?

The presumption of law is that if you are under seven, you cannot be criminally responsible. If you're over seven and under 12, you are responsible only if you understand what you are doing. That is a protection for the child. Above 12, the law gives no special protection against liability. However, although the punishment may be different, and the procedures may be different, the welfare of the child remains paramount. The whole point is to give the child an opportunity to reform. The problem arises when the child does not take the opportunity to reform.

Take the current problem we have with loan sharks and runners for loan sharks. Some of them are 12 years old. We drag them in, we try not to punish them, we give them a chance and if they reform they go into adult life, hopefully having learnt from the experience to keep out of these kinds of things; but some of them do not. They are incorrigible, the problem is intractable, they do it again, they join a secret society, they do harassment, they push drugs, they are involved in money laundering, and what do we do? Do we say, as it were, *okay, all your youthful indiscretions below the age of 16, we forget those*? When they have taken the chance to reform, we shouldn't hold it against them. But when they haven't taken the chance, the opportunity to reform, then this should be a relevant consideration in sentencing. The prosecution, the investigation agencies, the judges, all have a wider responsibility to society. We can't just say we will treat an adult as if it's his first offence and let him out after two weeks in jail, if actually he has had 10 previous similar offences; because if he does it again, how are you going to apologise to the victims?

— From the Question & Answer session

That's part of the problem. Infancy now denotes something else. In the good old days, Oxbridge undergrads who were under 21 were considered infants. They could get away with not paying for things like fancy waistcoats. Nowadays at 18, they are fully adults. My boys are now in university and one of their classmates went to America. She said she was surprised that 80% of her group in the United States are no longer virgins. At least they claimed not to be. And since we haven't cross-examined them, we have to take it at face value. But you see, the point is that morals have changed. I would say a generation ago, you wouldn't boast about that. You would keep it quiet, or mention it only within a small circle of friends.

But the idea of sexual activities by children shouldn't surprise us. How many of you, I wonder, have read the book *Wild Swans* by Jung Chang?[2] She wrote this bestseller about her experience and that of her mother and grandmother in China from the fall of the Qing dynasty in 1911 to the Cultural Revolution. Three generations of Chinese women. Jung Chang's grandmother was born in 1909, and became a concubine of a warlord in Beijing in 1924. You do the maths, she was about 15 at the time, and obviously he didn't take her in to put her through school, once she was his concubine.

You might remember *Romeo and Juliet*? Juliet's father Capulet says that she hasn't seen the change of 14 years. In other words, she's 13 at the time. So, this idea that kids shouldn't be sexually active seems to be a fairly recent phenomenon. If anything, we seem to be reverting to an earlier age; but the law still looks at those under 16 as children, to be precise. And the protection the law gives here, it gives mostly to girls. For some reason, the boys don't seem to be equally deserving of protection and very often they are considered to be perpetrators rather than victims.

Let me take you through some of the provisions, just to set the background. We have the Penal Code section 375 sub-section (d) — this was before 2008; after 2008, the sections were

---

[2] Jung Chang, *Wild Swans* (New York: Globalflair Ltd/Simon & Schuster, 1991).

recast following the British model. It didn't make them any clearer; the old model we had was Indian which frankly was better, but there it is, we follow the British provisions. The old section 375 (d) made sexual intercourse with girls under 14 illegal, with or without consent. In popular terms, this is called statutory rape. If she was married, however, it wasn't rape unless she was under 13. So you could have sex with your wife, if she was 13 even though she was under 14. You might ask, why 13? It was because in common law, a girl under 13 could not give consent to sexual intercourse. After 2008, this was recast. The word sexual intercourse was replaced with vaginal penetration — I'm not sure if that's an improvement. The section was increased in length but the basic concept remains. Under 14, no sex even with consent, unless the girl is a wife. Under 13, absolutely no.

Then we have the Women's Charter; carnal connection with a girl under 16. This is section 140 sub-section 1 (i). It's again an offence, unless the perpetrator has a reasonable belief that the girl was 16 or above. So there is a reasonable belief defence. But for statutory rape, reasonable belief is not a defence. The law is, again, protecting only girls, so it's not gender-neutral.

Then we have the Children and Young Persons Act section 7, sexual exploitation of a child under 14, or a young person who is over 14 but under 16. Whoever commits an obscene or indecent act on the child or the young person has committed an offence. This one is gender-neutral, so the victim can be a girl or a boy.

In 2008, there was a whole new set of offences introduced, including section 376A, which covers sexual penetration of a minor under 16, and this again is gender-neutral; also 376B, commercial sex with a minor under 18, again both girls and boys. For these two offences, the defence of reasonable mistake as to the age of the victim is not available unless the perpetrator is under 21 and has not been previously convicted. The philosophy, as you see, is to treat these young people as the victims. And in the case of the under-18s, to the under-16s through to 14, consent is a possible defence. Mistake as to age is a possible defence, but below 14 it's not a defence.

PROTECTING CHILDREN FROM THEMSELVES?

> **If a girl who is under 14 is involved in sexual activity, might there be a presumption of inadequate guardianship? Could we suggest an amendment to require an investigation under the Care and Protection Order made by the court in such cases?**
>
> These girls are treated as victims, as far as the law is concerned. As to whether or not there should be some responsibility on the part of the caregiver, here we are moving into a different field. Whether it is desirable to actually impose a legal liability — this is something that I would hesitate to give a quick answer to. It's something that we need to study, so that we get it right. It's a decision that we would need societal consensus on. I'm being very cautious because it's very easy to give a quick answer now, and regret it later, as what we write into the law will remain in force until we change the law again.
>
> — *From the Question & Answer session*

This worked when there was a societal consensus that sex took place within the confines of marriage, and since in Singapore the minimum age is 18 unless you get a special license from the minister, it meant basically that underage sex would be fairly rare. Rare not in the sense that it didn't happen. Rare in the sense that people wouldn't report it.

Because what we see from the figures is not the frequency of the offences, obviously. What we see is the frequency of reporting the offences. And a generation ago, I would suspect that there were many families who would keep this kind of thing quiet, rather than approach the police; which would mean a big fuss, appearing in the court and having newspapers and reporters there looking for salacious details. But nowadays, things have changed somewhat.

Some of you might remember *Tammy*. Does that ring any bells? It is a series of films in the early 1960s, it started off with Debbie Reynolds, and then Sandra Dee took over. Very innocent, she lived on a riverboat with her grandfather and she fell in love with practically every man that came her way. It is very chaste and very innocent. But in Singapore, I think a lot of people might remember the 2006 incident of the "Tammy" video; this Tammy was a polytechnic student, 17 years old, who filmed herself having sex with her boyfriend, and it got onto the internet. That's what has happened in 40 years; Tammy has changed quite a bit in the last 40 years. The sexual revolution in the West, I think, has finally reached us. In the West, they started in the 1960s. We don't have as much literature, as much media or film as they do, but you can see it happening.

If you are interested in film, you can look back. In the 1980s there was a film called *Little Darlings*. I don't know if any of you remember that. It was a very forgettable film, except it had two young stars, Tatum O'Neal and Kristy McNichol, and it starred these two 15-year-old teenagers at summer camp, who made a bet as to who will lose her virginity first. That was the 1980s; it never came

Source: *The Straits Times* © Singapore Press Holdings Limited. Reprinted with permission.

to Singapore. The interesting thing about *Little Darlings* is that when they showed it on American television they took out all the sexual references, so it became a story about them betting on who would fall in love first, which is not quite the same. Now, nearly 30 years after the film was made, they restored everything and no one was shocked, because the attitudes have changed. And the attitudes have changed even in Singapore.

If you read our newspapers, they've been reporting figures in the last few months. *Today* paper on the 12th of October 2009 reported that 310 girls under 16 were caught for engaging in consensual sex last year, up from 216 in 2007 and five years ago it was only 163. These are the ones that were caught; heaven knows how many were uncaught. *The Straits Times*, 8th August, statutory rape; consensual sex cases were 37 in the first half of 2009, as opposed to 21 in the first half of 2008. These figures are actually from the police crime brief. So the numbers have increased somewhat. It's not as if this is a problem that is confined only to the West.

If you read our newspapers, you'll see that practically every week we've got something about somebody having sex with an under-age child. In many of these cases, it is very obvious that these people deserved to be prosecuted. We also have incest cases, which unfortunately seem to be on the rise, just judging anecdotally from the kinds of things that come to my desk. I should say that I don't see every case; it's physically impossible to do that. With 14,000 police reports a year, it's impossible to review them all. Deputy public prosecutors would process the cases and only the most serious cases will come to me. So I say anecdotally, that I have seen more cases. I'm seeing more cases of sexual relations with children under 14, with girls under 16. These things are coming up; just picking up yesterday's newspaper, another report of an under-14 sex case. It's there; it's a problem.

The figures, of course, reveal a change in the mores of society, the understanding of what is acceptable, and what is unacceptable, and one sees speculation in the media that this has something to

The source of the problem could be increased sexual awareness of children brought about by the internet. Are there laws against undesirable websites, as in China?

We have laws that allow us to prosecute in cases where there is pornography, to prosecute in cases where there are undesirable publications. But we use a very light touch. China may want to build a great wall around the internet, but it's not possible. People will find a way around. I'm sure the same criticisms were made when radio arrived, when television was invented. The problem is not the media; the problem is that the moral codes have changed.

Hollywood used to have a code of conduct where, apparently, if you saw two actors in bed, each of them would have to have one foot on the ground, just so that you could be sure there was no hanky-panky. That code seems to have gone. So I would say for the internet, build a great wall if you like, build a Maginot Line if you like, but remember the barbarians got through the Great Wall and the Germans worked around the Maginot Line. The law is not a Maginot Line. We will not hesitate to prosecute if there is an offence. But we have too few prosecutors to monitor the internet and I'm sure the police have better things to do, enjoyable as it may be to surf all day.

— *From the Question & Answer session*

do with the internet and films and television, and I am sure we can't discount this. But whatever the causes are, the fact is that children nowadays seem to be more open about their sexuality and more willing to experiment. I have divided the cases involving children into four different categories.

We have one set of cases where the victim consents and one set where the victim does not consent. And then we have a set of cases where the perpetrator is an adult, in the sense that he is over 18, and the other set where he is not an adult, in the sense that he is under 18. I use "he" purely for convenience because we do get "shes" as perpetrators as well.

The clearest cases, category one, are where the perpetrators are adults and the victim does not consent. That is not a problem. I think we will have a complete consensus that there should be a prosecution and the court should come down hard. In some of these cases, we have multiple assaults over a period of time. In a distressing number of cases, it is a family member, often the father. And these are cases that are most distressing to prosecute, because you see a pattern of abuse from when the child was five or six, and in extreme cases it leads to death. And it is emotionally taxing to prosecute these. But we have no problem with the idea of prosecuting these cases.

Then we have the next category of cases, where the perpetrator is an adult, but the victim consents. This is a bit more problematic because there are adults and there are adults. You have an 18-year-old boy with 15-year-old girlfriend; do you treat this the same as a 60-year-old man with a 14-year-old girl? There is a whole range out there. But as a general rule, these are cases that we would prosecute. We assume that if you are 18 years old, you know what you are doing and you know jolly well that if the girl is below 16, don't do it. So normally, these cases we would prosecute. We have discretion and when the discretion is exercised, we agonise over cases like this. But generally speaking, we will bring them to court.

Let me explain one thing at this point . The prosecutor's job is not to decide what punishment is appropriate. The prosecutor's job is to decide whether or not the case should go to court so that the judge can look at the evidence, reach a verdict, then decide what is appropriate. But if we decide not to prosecute, it means the judge would never even have the chance to look at the case. We would just be going to let the fellow off.

But I should say, we don't just let the fellow off. We introduced something that we call a conditional warning, which means in certain cases, we tell the person that, "we are not going to prosecute you this time, but if in the next year or two years, whatever period we stipulate, if you get into trouble again like this, we will prosecute you for the new offence and this present one too". This gives an incentive to the person to keep clean. But it also gives him a chance because there is no record, no prosecution; there is no charge. We hold it in abeyance. That is how the prosecutorial discretion works.

The third category is where you have the accused who is under 18 and the victim does not consent. Now these are cases where, again, generally we would prosecute because if the victim does not consent, why should it make a difference whether or not the accused is over 18 or under 18? However, again it is not as straightforward as that. I've had a case of a 14-year-old boy who was charged with rape of the family maid. A 14-year-old. We prosecuted him. The difficult decision concerns what the judge can do with him. It is a clear case of rape, 14 years old and family maid. So you do have sexual predators who are aged 14, who are even younger than 14 and we have to bring these people to the court because we can't just say, "you don't do this again". We are responsible. If they do it again, who is going to apologise to the victim and her family? So we bring it to the court and the judge has to make a decision. These also are relatively straightforward in terms of prosecutorial discretion. Where there is no consent, it is going to take a lot to persuade us not to bring it to court.

Then we have the final category which is the most difficult. Victim consents, accused is under 18. We've got a situation where it's basically kids having sex. Now, why is this a problem? I'm sure we are all familiar with this kind of situation, where we have young people, their hormones are raging and they are watching television. They watch American television; and even prime time American television now takes it for granted that casual sex is acceptable. These are the messages they get. There are British TV series about school kids where they take it for granted that sex is acceptable. Not just acceptable, but inevitable!

My boys were educated abroad in an international school. There was a lot of angst and agonising among their friends around 14 or 15 because they did not have a girlfriend, and they would think: *What's wrong with me? Am I hideous? Will I never reproduce? Will my genes die out?* That sort of angst. They came back to Singapore to do their junior college studies. Junior college in Singapore is totally different from school overseas. Everyone is obsessed with grades. Once the exams are over, *then* the hormones burst out. But before the exams it's very chaste, not the same as in Europe.

But I think in some of the schools, again just anecdotally from the cases that come to me, they do have these problems. These things matter, and not only in the physical sense. People fancy they're in love. People have relations because it seems to be socially necessary to maintain position. And it's not an old phenomenon; Romeo and Juliet, as I said, the girl's 13. You are familiar with the Chinese legend, *Liang Zhu*? The butterfly lovers? The girl was barely in her teens. She disguised herself as a boy to be a scholar, and fell in love with another scholar. This legend dates from the Eastern Jin dynasty, which is about 500 years after the

Three Kingdoms and the unification of China; it's well over a thousand years old. It is not a new problem; it is a thousand-year-old problem that we have. It's just that with television we have much more exposure.

What do you do in a case like this where the couple think they are in love? It is not so bad when people don't think they are in love. You have a situation where two kids, they are experimenting, things get out of hand and, you know, the boy takes advantage of the girl even though she consents. It is a bit easier to decide to prosecute then. The problem is less easy when the girl consents and then later has a change of mind or the parents find out, which is why the girl has a change of mind, very often. And then you get a report made.

The worst cases, of course, are where the girl actually entices the boy. This is not uncommon. In the last year and half that I've been Attorney-General, I have seen at least three cases where the girl initiated the contact. There was one where I think the record stated that she had eight boyfriends. She started at 11; she stopped when she got pregnant. We can't name people; we need to protect not the innocent but the guilty. There are cases like this. They go on the internet, they meet at the chat rooms, they meet on whatever it is, Facebook or Friendster, and get to know one another. They decide to have some physical contact. One thing leads to another and then we have statutory rape. The boy gets reported; the boy has committed an offence.

What do we do in a case like that? This is the prosecutors' nightmare. In most of these cases, if it is the boy's first time, we normally warn. Normally. But every case has to be considered on its facts. Warning the boy is not always satisfactory to the so-called "victims". I use "victim" in inverted commas because in these cases, they are not really victims. They are willing participants. Warning the boy very often doesn't satisfy the parents of the so-called victims who sometimes feel they have lost face or that we are letting the young villain get away with things.

We had one case where the girl ran away from home, to be with the boyfriend. She was 14 at the time, went off with her boyfriend, they had sex. And the father finally got her back, reported the boy and because it was the first time, because they had a relationship, we didn't prosecute. The police gave a warning and that was that. And then she ran away again, back to the same boy, who should have known better. He went off with her, she was just shy of 16, and had sex with her. This time we prosecuted. The boy went to jail because it wasn't the first time. You can't sympathise with him just because they fancied they were in love. I don't know whether it will work out, but that is what they think: they are in a relationship. The father of the girl was actually very upset. He even wrote to his MP. He said, "How could you let this fellow off the first time; see what he did the second time? He got my daughter pregnant." As if it was all the boy's fault and he, the father, has no responsibility for her at all. The girl ran away from her family, but the father still felt outraged that the boy had been treated lightly.

We had another case, of two youngsters in Secondary Two, one a foreigner, in a relationship. The girl got pregnant, so again, a police report was made. There was a settlement among the families. The boy's parents, who were foreigners, would pay for all the expenses of the pregnancy. They would even have the child adopted. So that was settled. It seemed to be okay. But for some reason the girl's parents changed their mind and so it came back again to Chambers, and in a case like this, again we warned the boy. What else could we do? Send a 15-year-old boy to jail? What good would that do? And this is the problem that we have with the law. When you have a consensual relationship, what good would it do to send the boy to jail, to give him a record? Yet to let him go off with a warning seems to be unsatisfactory to the other side.

It is not just us that grapple with these problems. The British also do because they have a tidal wave of promiscuity. This year, if I'm not mistaken, is the first time most children are born outside formal marriage. So they've had this problem and they have grappled with it. To them it is a question of human rights; to us it is a matter of simple law and order. But the challenges are still the same.

Let me read something from Baroness Hale about statutory rape, because she has a rather interesting way of putting things. This is Baroness Hale in the House of Lords, a 2008 case, talking about statutory rape.[3] Why is it an offence, a crime? In fact in England you can go to jail for life for statutory rape, not that they do ever send anyone to jail for life.

She says,

> ... This is because the law regards the attitude of the victim of this behaviour as irrelevant to the commission of the offence (although it may, of course, be relevant to the appropriate sentence).

In other words, whether the girl consents or not is irrelevant to the crime but it is relevant to the sentencing of the accused.

> Even if a child is fully capable of understanding and freely agreeing to such sexual activity, which may often be doubted, especially with a child under 13, the law says that it makes no difference. He or she is legally disabled from consenting.

So this is the attitude of English law, and this is the attitude of our law, too.

> It is important to stress that the object is not only to protect such children from predatory adult paedophiles but also to protect them from premature sexual activity of all kinds. They are protected in two ways: first, by the fact that it is irrelevant whether or not they want or appear to want it; and secondly, by the fact that in the case of children under 13 it is irrelevant whether or not the possessor of the penis in question knows the age of the child he is penetrating.

> Thus, there is not strict liability in relation to the conduct involved. The perpetrator has to intend to penetrate. Every male has a choice about where he puts his penis. It may be difficult for him to restrain himself when aroused but he has a choice. There

---

[3] UKHL Judgments — *R v G* (Appellant) [2008 at 44 & 46].

is nothing unjust or irrational about a law which says that if that he chooses to put his penis inside a child who turns out to be under 13 he has committed an offence (although the state of his mind may again be relevant to sentence). He also commits an offence if he behaves in the same way towards a child of 13 but under 16, albeit only if he does not reasonably believe that the child is 16 or over. So in principle sex with a child under 16 is not allowed. When the child is under 13, three years younger than that, he takes the risk that she may be younger than he thinks she is. The object is to make him take responsibility for what he chooses to do with what is capable of being, not only an instrument of great pleasure, but also a weapon of great danger.

To end, I want to mention a few other difficult cases. A boy who was 15 decided that his pocket money wasn't sufficient to maintain the sort of lifestyle that he would like. So he went on to the internet, to gay chat rooms, and basically advertised himself. Six men contacted him and had sexual relations with this 15-year-old boy. All six were prosecuted; they pleaded guilty. There were no doubts; the evidence was overwhelming. We reduced the charges in many of the cases, because this was a case where the boy was actually selling himself. So it is not just girls; it's also boys.

These are things that we need to deal with. It is not easy for the court to deal with a situation like this; it is very difficult. This is not likely to be the last case of this sort. In the past, we very often had old men and young girls, and I think the societal consensus was *throw the book at them, slam the jail cell door, forget that they were ever there*. But now we have cases of older women and young boys. We have seen two cases in the last year alone. Now the point about this is that the young boy has to consent, since it is very difficult for the older woman to force him, and I'm willing to bet he enjoyed the process. But we still prosecute her. We have to prosecute her. And in one case, the first case that came up, the reason that it actually came up was because the boy got possessive and started making threats. The woman got worried and made a police report and everything came out. So the 'Mrs Robinsons' have to be very careful, be careful of whom they pick.

Does the law take into consideration an accused person's intellectual ability when prosecuting?

Yes, we absolutely do take that into account in deciding whether it's appropriate to prosecute or whether it's better to let the accused off with a warning. The judge takes that into account because when we prosecute, very often what the prosecutor does is say, in effect, *these are the facts, but we're not pressing for a hard sentence. We're bringing it to court because there's a public interest in ensuring this comes out in public.*

If the prosecutor does not press for a hard sentence, the judge can take the cue, and he knows that the prosecution is not going to appeal if he gives a lighter sentence. But we have to be very careful about this. Just because a person is intellectually challenged doesn't necessarily mean he cannot distinguish right from wrong. Intellectual incapacity or psychiatric problems we take into account. There is no general rule beyond the fact that we will look at it and if it's a genuine case then we'll look at it sympathetically. That doesn't mean we wouldn't prosecute, but we'll be sympathetic.

— From the Question & Answer session

This particular case I mentioned about the older woman, the first case, was very interesting because there was a great difference in opinion within Chambers. It was quite clear that we had to prosecute her. The problem was should we ask for custodial sentence, and, if so, how long? Because you see, as a prosecutor we have to give some sort of indication to the judge whether it's just a fining offence, or whether the offender should be let off with a slap on the wrist or whatever it is. So sometimes we have great difference in opinion, and, strangely enough, the male prosecutors were more inclined to go easy on the woman. The female prosecutors — without meaning to generalise — were much more willing to throw her into jail for a long period.

But this illustrates the type of problems that we face. The bottom line is that whether we like it or not, society's morals have changed. The law remains rooted in a 19th- and 20th-century morality, and the prosecution is bound by those laws, because we cannot change them, we can only work with a framework. The law is a very blunt instrument when we are dealing with category four cases: young boy meets young girl, there is consent. The most that we can do is to bring it to the judge in court and hope that he can find a solution that is good for all the parties. It is not easy and this is where the non-governmental organisations, the community services, play a part. Obviously the decision is not just for the judge. The judge cannot do very much alone. There has to be some follow-up.

Even if you send the boy or the girl to jail, or both of them to jail, there's got to be something done. Sending them to jail *per se* won't make them reflect on their lives. That's the last thing that's going to happen. But for good or ill this is the framework that we have. It is the framework that we will keep. It is the framework that we will enforce. The traditional deterrence that underlines our penal law does not quite work in category four cases. You're never going to convince teenagers that what they were doing is wrong. They may know it. They may feel it. But in many cases, they actually think they are Romeo and Juliet. They think they are in love. The world does not matter. And the last thing they are thinking of is the Penal Code, frankly.

CHAPTER FOUR

From Generation to Generation: Growing Up in Singapore

Aline Wong

About the Speaker

Dr Aline Wong, academic, politician and advocate for gender equality, is a sociologist by training with a long and distinguished academic and political career. She has been Academic Advisor to the SIM University since 2005, where she performs a consulting role in charting the strategic plan, establishing linkages with reputable local and overseas institutions, and providing advice on curriculum plans, including course and programme development. Before accepting the position at SIM University, Dr Wong was Chairman of the HDB Board from 2003 to 2007, and before that she was Professor and Senior Advisor to the President's Office in the National University of Singapore, from 2001 to 2003. She is also an adjunct faculty member of the Lee Kuan Yew School of Public Policy.

Dr Wong holds an Honorary Doctorate from Wheelock College, Boston, Massachusetts; PhD and Master's degrees in Sociology from the University of California, Berkeley; and a BA in Economics and Political Science from the University of Hong Kong. She pursued her academic career at NUS where she became a full Professor in 1990.

In 1984, Dr Wong entered politics and was elected Member of Parliament at four successive General Elections. From 1990 to 1994, she was Minister of State for Health and Education, and became Senior Minister of State in 1995. She held that position until she stepped down from politics in 2001 and returned to NUS.

Dr Wong is also a Founding Member of the Singapore Women's Initiative for Ageing Successfully (WINGS). She was a Director of MediaCorp Pte Ltd and the Singapore Symphonia Company, and the President of the International Women's Forum (Singapore Chapter).

Reflecting on her lecture at the end of 2014, Dr Wong reiterated and elaborated her concerns. Misperceptions arise, she pointed out, because of generational differences. And there is nowadays so much overlap in age, from the very young to the very old, all active and in contact, that it is more obvious when there is a clash of values or expectations. We now live in a much more intergenerational world, as the generations are in the public domain, and are not just a matter of an extended family of three or four generations in one compound.

However, as she noted throughout her lecture, existing analyses of generational differences are based on western studies and rely on the impact of events that were often far more significant for the West and especially the United States than for Asia in general, still less Singapore in particular.

Of course some events — like the Financial Crises 1997 and 2008 — were global, with a big local impact too, but, really, what affects and shapes the generations in Singapore are actually local events much more than global events. We can only understand ourselves through an analysis of local events, what Dr Wong describes as "signposts" for each generation. But as a tiny nation, we need to look beyond ourselves and be aware of what is happening and impacting us elsewhere.

The hugely energetic and animated Dr Wong — herself of a generation, born in 1941, that "straddled" the war — is still keenly interested in contemporary events and issues affecting the younger generation. It is important, she feels, to be aware of what younger generations see as success and failure. Maybe we now need more emphasis on giving children practical job-oriented skills. There are more roads to success than just academic ones, she concludes.

Aline Wong in 1952

The 4ᵗʰ Lecture, delivered 6 November 2010

When Mr Koh Choon Hui, Singapore Children's Society Chairman, invited me to give the fourth SCS Lecture, I hesitated. Because, though I have taught family sociology a long time ago, children's issues are not my forte. But on reflection, I said I'll give it a try, because recently I have been reflecting on differences in generations, and on intergenerational relationships. I had attended some public lectures offered by management consultants at SIM University, where they talked about generations in the western context; and they used their observations on trends to tell us Singaporeans what our generations are like as well. So Mr Koh's invitation really goaded me to look into the evidence, to come to a more precise understanding, locally, of what the generations are really like here in Singapore, and what this implies for intergeneration relations.

My talk will consist of four parts. The first part deals with some general concepts and some of the difficulties involved in pinning down what the generations are. The second will summarise what the western literature has said about the characteristics of Generations X, Y, Z plus the Baby Boomers. In the third part, I will try to find the Singapore context for these or similar generations locally, and how we would describe them. And finally, I will say something about Generation Y in Singapore now — people who are in their late 20s and perhaps early 30s — and some of their characteristics and the challenges they face.

General Concepts: Life Cycle Stages, Childhood, and What Defines a Generation

General ideas about a person's life cycle stages are very familiar to everyone; from birth to infancy to childhood to adolescence or youth, adulthood, middle age and old age. But actually, these stages are not just a matter of biological facts alone. How do you define childhood? What is childhood? How do you define adolescence, who are the youths, and what are they supposed to be doing at their stage of life? And who is an adult, and at what point do you become middle-aged? Such questions and such concepts are not biological alone. They are based on the social and cultural meanings we attach to these groups of people; what they are supposed to be doing for society, for you, for me and for themselves.

It turns out, during the historical course of development of society, from agrarian to pre-industrial to industrial to post-industrial society, that the kinds of ways we look at and value children have changed over the centuries. In 1962, Philippe Ariès published a very famous French study called *Centuries of Childhood*.[1] He talked about the way children were depicted in medieval history, in literature, journals, paintings and art. And he inferred that in those times, people apparently did not have a distinct idea of what childhood is, of what children are. This may sound very strange to you. But if you look at his sources, children are depicted as little adults. And if you go back, and look at our own black and white fading family photos, not too long ago, you find children very dressed up, very solemn, standing in a row with their parents, and they look like little adults too. Of course, this is only for appearances, and Ariès has been criticised for the kind of source materials he used. Plus he was not scientific in his sampling and used only those children belonging to the aristocratic class. Nevertheless, you can see what he meant if you consider what we know of the ordinary people, the people on farms or in the countryside.

There is no doubt in agrarian societies and pre-industrial societies, where the vast majority of the populations grew up in the countryside, children had lots of responsibilities. As soon as they could, maybe around the age of seven or eight, children were expected to help on the farm. They were expected to fetch wood, fetch water, tend to chickens, tend to buffalos, and so on, and also take care of younger siblings. They had these responsibilities, which is work! So, childhood, as a period such as we know it now,

---

[1] Philippe Ariès, *Centuries of Childhood: A Social History of Family Life* (New York: Random House, 1962). Translated from the French, *L'Enfant et la vie familiale sous l'ancien regime*.

when children should be allowed to be happy, to enjoy themselves and we should indulge them — that kind of conceptualisation is very recent. It happens only after society has advanced to a
certain level of affluence. One that requires students to be
schooled full-time, and not just be going to school in the morning
as in rural villages in China nowadays, when children may need to
walk one or two miles to the village school and still do farm work
in the afternoon.

With modernisation of society, then, the conceptualisation and
also the value of children changes. What do we mean by "value"?
Value of course has an economic connotation, and you can find out
the kinds of cost involved in bringing up a child: feeding, clothing,
schooling, providing for toys, recreation, holidays, and so on.
Added together, you soon find a pretty daunting economic cost
entailed in bringing up a child. That is one of the reasons why many
modern parents think about the economics of having children.

So children have monetary costs. They also incur opportunity costs
for the parents, meaning the mother may not be able to work or
work full-time outside the home, or the father may not be able to
do all the kinds of things he would want to do if he were not a
father. Of course, children do also bring a value in life satisfaction.
I won't say a sense of immortality, but the sense of extension of
oneself. I mean, see how parents look for similarities in the features
of their newborn baby. "Ah! This is me!" This is the mother, all seen
in this little baby. So the sense of extension of one's self, life satisfaction, and children bring a lot of emotional warmth to the family.
But in former days, children were valued not only because they
added a pair of working hands, but they also provided security for
the parents in old age. So beneath a veneer, the idea of children as
children, are ideas about the economic value of children.

Let me turn briefly to the question of why the "generation problem" is a problem. Societies go through demographic transitions,
from having high birth rates to low birth rates. Many societies are
facing an ageing population now.

However, it is not just population ageing that is at the root of the so-called generation problem. It is also because people live much longer nowadays, so that we have the older generations which are still around while their children are having children themselves. We have multiple overlapping generations.

In the old days children were considered to be a return on investment. The transfer of wealth was initially from parents to children. When parents grew old, children gave back to parents. But nowadays, things are beginning to change. I am not saying there is a lot of evidence, but research in western societies does show grandparents are involved in giving financial help, emotional help, all kinds of practical help to their children and their children's children. So the intergeneration transfer cycle has been changed and as far as social policies are concerned, there is a big debate going on as a result, on matters like healthcare reforms, social security, pension systems. Who pays for the elderly? For care for them in old age? How much tax should be levied on the young people, so that we can carry what is called the old-age dependency ratio in the population? People have said this will lead to intergenerational conflicts, a breaking of the intergenerational contract.

So we are living longer. We are getting healthier, we are getting better educated, and we want to remain active for longer periods of time. In the old days, many grandchildren did not get to see or interact with their full set of four grandparents, because some of them would have died when their grandchildren were born or when their children were growing up. But now, you have multiple generations who are alive and well, interacting and supporting each other.

At the workplace, many people above 60, 65, are still working. You may even have four generations. Generations X, Y and Z people who are just in their teens, are working along with the "uncles" and "aunties" in McDonalds. In the office, your boss may be someone who is very much older and experienced, but who may not understand your ways of working. This has given rise to quite a bit of management literature on how people of different ages should adapt to each other and how their work styles are different in the same workplace, and how they should manage the intergenerational differences.

These intergeneration issues present a whole new social frontier. To be of theoretical relevance, a generation refers to people born in a certain place at a certain time. Although each individual is unique, we all share similarities because we grew up in very similar circumstances and environments, when we were young and impressionable, and still forming our beliefs and attitudes towards the world. So, a generation is not just a biological phenomenon. A generation has a sociological definition. A generation is defined as a group, a cohort, of individuals born and living contemporaneously, who have common knowledge and experiences that affect their thoughts, attitudes, values, beliefs and behaviours.[2]

---

[2] This definition is from Meagan Johnson and Larry Johnson, *Generations, Inc.: From Boomers to Linksters — Managing the Friction between Generations at Work* (New York: American Management Association, 2010).

Now, what are these common experiences and knowledge? We can think of them as signposts or significant public events that happen around the time that you are growing up. These signposts, like road signs, point to future directions. You can go in one direction because of these signposts, or you could have gone in another direction. These are significant events that affect you, affect the society and affect the world.

Now, if a generation is not just a biological phenomenon, but is also a social, economic, political and cultural phenomenon, then how long is a generation? As the age of marriage gets higher, the age of childbearing gets later. We also live longer. So you would think the length of a generation is increasing. But in fact, the length of a generation is being compressed, becoming shorter and shorter. With rapid change in technology, with global communications and globalisation of culture and values, we become exposed to many more significant happenings around the world, at a very fast speed. In the past, 25 years probably defined a generation. Now, it is probably 15.

What are these significant events that impact and shape a defined generation? Looking through the literature, I think there is quite a range of significant things. Economic cycles, war and conflict, education and advancement, technological revolutions, changing women's status, changing family structures. And there are the popular culture and lifestyle changes. Everyone seems to be affected by popular culture and the media. Popular culture and lifestyle changes are also major forces that define a generation.

What Are Generations X Y Z?

"Generations" are generalisations, based sometimes on scientific studies, sometimes on anecdotes, sometimes on perceptions that may not be so precise. But they are generalisations which are useful for spotting trends. They have been used for understanding intergenerational relationships in broad terms, and also for mass communications and mass marketing. The marketing people actually target certain generations for certain products and services, so they have been using this concept in a big way. The problem is that, when you divide the generations, there are people who were born in between these generations, who "straddle" them, so how do you classify them?

Of the generations I shall mention, the most famous in the 20th century is the Baby Boomer generation. These are the people born between 1946 and 1964 because there was a baby boom right after World War II. Soldiers returned home, economic conditions stabilised and the western economy took off. There was growing prosperity, so people felt secure and started having children. Consequently there was a bulge in the population of the United States and other western societies after World War II. The parents of these Baby Boomers we call the Traditionals, or sometimes Depression babies; they had endured the Great Depression and the war, and then benefitted from the post-war economic growth. But the Baby Boomers themselves grew up during a 1960s period of social causes and revolutions followed by the disappointing 1970s, when there were recessions, reversals of causes, the Vietnam War and economic stagnation. This is the so-called Baby Boomer generation.

After the Baby Boomers, there is the Generation X who were born from 1965 to 1980. Generation Y follows, born between 1981 and 1995. The mid-1990s are significant because of the very fast spread of the internet. Generation Y is actually the computer generation, the internet generation. Other than that, these dates seem to be arbitrary, but they are not so arbitrary if you think about them. Generation Z arrives after about 1995, but people do not use the term Z very much yet. I don't think it is stated very clearly anywhere what Generation Z is. We are still talking about Generation Y.

But how do we begin to understand the generations more precisely? There are certain research issues. Should we use the year of birth or the growing up years? The growing up years make more sense, they are formative years in terms of values, attitudes and one's world view. But it is an assumption that what happens out

I'm a Baby Boomer. Singapore is changing fast in terms of landscapes. The street where I grew up is no longer around. When signposts which existed when we were younger are no longer around, how does this impact old people, the Traditional generation?

It's a very good question. Singapore has been developing very fast. And in the beginning, I think we were destroying too many old sites, on which people hung their sentiments and memories. But it was not entirely a matter of our tearing down things too fast at the beginning. It is also that Singapore has had a very short history. There have been no thousands of years to accumulate culture. And the kind of things that were inherited from colonial times were not always sufficiently sophisticated, that we would say they should be preserved. Nevertheless, beginning in the late 1980s, the government, and Mr Dhanabalan especially, made great efforts to preserve and conserve urban spaces and buildings. Now, as people grow older, they become more nostalgic. And with an increasing ageing population this will become quite significant for society.

When things change too fast, there are no familiar landmarks. Constant pushing forward is bound to affect our national psyche, but just how I don't know. And it will be a great loss if we think we must always be pushing on and on without thinking about relationships and associations with the places that form our home.

— *From the Question & Answer session*

there in the world, or what happens in the region, impacts you and produces changes in you. And, even for the same generations, there are inconsistencies among different authors.

How do you choose a signpost and the categorisation to characterise a generation? I have listed the signposts[3] for the Baby

---

[3] Following Johnson & Johnson (2010), already cited. Other sources offer similar lists.

Boomers below. As you can see, these signposts are very "western-centric", and Singaporeans may not necessarily relate to the events mentioned, which did not happen on our soil. There will be a need to contextualise what we mean by generations locally, which I will come to later.

1960	John F Kennedy is elected
1961–2	Bay of Pigs Invasion, Cuban Missile Crisis (almost a US/USSR nuclear war)
1963	John F Kennedy is assassinated
1968	• Martin Luther King, Jr. & Robert Kennedy are assassinated • Chicago Democratic Convention riots
1969	• Janis Joplin & Jimmy Hendrix die (famous US pop musicians) • Man walks on the moon (the space race) • Woodstock Music & Art Fair is held
1973	Watergate scandal
1974	• Richard Nixon resigns • OPEC oil policy (a huge rate of inflation resulted, internationally and in Singapore)
1976	Jimmy Carter is elected
1979	Hostages are taken in Iran
1980	• Ronald Reagan is elected • Iran hostages are released • John Lennon is assassinated
1984	Macintosh is introduced

Baby Boomers were born between 1946 and 1964. Among the most famous things about them, you may remember, in the 1960s, were the student movements, the civil rights movement and the anti-Vietnam war protest movement, all of which were said to be revolutionary and had a big imprint on young people and their attitudes towards life then.

Now, based on this set of signposts, the western Baby Boomers were said to be youthful, idealistic, desiring to change the world, sceptical towards authority, meaning the government and civil institutions. They value individual achievement and recognition, are highly competitive and driven, and play by rules to win or climb the corporate ladder. They tend to view money as a symbol of competitive success and have a passion for life, for change and for meaning. They often marry late and have their children later in life, "wanting to do it right."

The next cohort is Generation X, born 1965 to 1980. Again, I have listed the signposts.[4]

1973	First cellular phone call
1978	Jonestown mass suicides (of cult leader & followers)
1981	Assassination attempt on Ronald Reagan
1986	*Challenger* disaster (failed space rocket launch)
1987	Stock market crash (Black Monday)
1988	Pan Am Flight 103 crash (planted bomb)
1989	• *Exxon Valdez* (oil tanker) spill • Fall of Berlin Wall
1990	Gulf War
1992	• Recession • Rodney King beating
1993	• Bill Clinton is elected (first Baby Boomer President) • Dotcom boom begins
1994	Death of Kurt Cobain (lead singer of rock band)
1995	OJ Simpson trial

What about the characteristics of Generation X? They grew up on a world stage which is now much quieter. But at home, in America, in the West, there were momentous changes in the family. In 1960, the United States Food and Drug Administration approved the commercial sale of the contraceptive pill. And that was part of the cause of the family revolution. Women became better educated, had higher labour force participation, lower birth rates and higher divorce rates. All this was affecting the family structure. An increasing proportion of children came from broken homes and they had foster kin. And adults and kids were facing social and economic insecurities because their parents went through the recession,

---

[4] Again from Johnson and Johnson (2010).

went through the stock market crash, and so on. And so, they had greater need for self-reliance. They were at the same time more disillusioned, cynical and apathetic towards government institutions. These people grew up along with the internet, when they were teens. When the Baby Boomers look at Generation X, the latter don't seem to be so hardworking, don't seem to be so committed to the work, though actually they are committed to the work but in a different manner. They want work to be engaging, fast-paced; they want to do their own thing; they want to be innovative. Generation X contributed such entrepreneurs as Bill Gates, Steve Jobs, people who were big inventors, big entrepreneurs, who thought out of the box.

I won't go over the signposts for Generation Y, born 1981 to 1985. Suffice it to say, they are also quite western-centric. But for Generation Y, technology comes naturally. These young people, they need to be always in touch; they seek groups; they do online social

Source: *The Straits Times* © Singapore Press Holdings Limited. Reprinted with permission.

networking. Their parents are so-called "helicopter" parents who are very solicitous towards their children. So Gen Y is the generation that grew up with all kinds of tuition and enrichment classes. This is the generation where some mothers can afford to stay home and take care of children full-time. There are a few fathers who also stay home and take care of children, full-time. They show emphasis on social responsibility, volunteerism and environmentalism.

The children, growing up under these circumstances, always seek approval and affirmation. At work, they always ask questions. They always want affirmation; they want instant responses from the bosses. *If I give you an idea, you better tell me whether it works or not. Give me a pattern and I'll show it to you I'm right, and tell me if I'm wrong.* They want instant feedback, constant interaction on the job. So at work, this Generation Y is also known as the "why" generation — "You tell me why I have to follow you".

To sum up these generations:

- Traditionals, "I want to join the world". Which means I want to work hard, earn money and keep up with the Joneses.
- Baby Boomers, "I want to help change the world". They don't want to follow the world, but eventually they do, though they still think they are changing the world.
- Generation X, "I need to keep my options open". I want to choose to work; I want to find an interesting job; I don't want to marry yet.
- Generation Y, "I need to live life now". I'll take time off; I'll go around the world. I want to find myself.

These are over-generalisations, but they may help to distinguish the generations.

The Singapore Context for These Generations

Now let's consider what was happening in Singapore. During these past 50 years or so, there has been rapid economic development in Singapore. Our population has grown from 1.6 million in 1960 to today's five million, with a sizeable proportion of foreigners. Our GDP per capita has risen from $1,330 in the 1960s to over $50,000 nowadays. There are tremendous changes, represented by economic growth, the physical transformation of our city, technological change, changes in the status of women and also family structure, and changes in the social values and orientation of our young people. So what are the generations in Singapore? Are there parallels with the West?

To answer these questions I took as my sourcebook *Chronicles of Singapore, 1959 to 2009* edited by Peter Lim, containing 50 years of headline news.[5] In order to find my significant events, I had to go back 50 years into the news. Peter Lim of course had his criteria for what counted as newsworthy, and I also have gone through the whole thing and noted down what seemed to me relevant for the comparison. Not every possible event is included, but I have picked what I judge were significant events locally and internationally from the headlines in the sourcebook, which was indeed an invaluable resource for this purpose. I have tabulated the results as comparisons, for each generation, showing both world events and Singapore events. So the next four tables show these comparisons, one table for each of the Traditional and Baby Boomer generations, plus Generations X and Y.

Table 1 shows these local and world events for the Traditional generation, who were born before the war. They lived through these, through the Japanese Occupation.

---

5   Peter H.L. Lim, ed., *Chronicles of Singapore — Fifty Years of Headline News 1959–2009*. (Singapore: Editions Didier-Millet, in association with the National Library Board, Singapore, 2010).

Table 1: Signposts for the Traditional generation, in Singapore and the world based on Lim, *Chronicles of Singapore, 1959 to 2009.*

World Events	Year	Events Relevant to Singapore
	1911	Republic of China is founded by Sun Yat Sen
WWI: *1914–1918*	1914	British colony, Straits Settlements, Federated Malay States, politics and economy tied to Malaya.
Great Depression	1929	Chinese considered China as home, sentiments favoured new China.
	1937	*1937–1945:* Japanese invasion of China
WWII: *1939–1945*	1939	
	1942	• *1942–1945:* Japanese Occupation of Singapore and Malaya • Roots of post-war independence movement and communist insurgency in Malaya are established
Second Chinese Civil War: *1945–1949*	1945	
	1948	British declare Malayan Emergency
	1949	People's Republic of China is founded by Mao Tse Tung
Korean War	1950	Tan Lark Sye proposes Nanyang University
	1953	Rendel Commission is appointed
	1954	• Labour Front administration • PAP is formed
• Swiss referendum rejects female suffrage • First picture of earth from space • Microchip is invented	1959	• Self-government • PAP landslide win • Lee Kuan Yew becomes first Prime Minister
	Early 1960s	• Law and order problems • Secret societies • Population explosion • Unemployment • Slums

Next we come to the Baby Boomers, whose formative years would be the early 1960s to the late 1970s. This is when Singapore achieved independence. Table 2 summarises the comparative signposts for this generation.

Table 2: Signposts for the Baby Boomers (born 1946–1964), in Singapore and the world, based on Lim, *Chronicles of Singapore, 1959 to 2009*.

World Events	Year	Events Relevant to Singapore
• USSR launches Sputnik 5 • OPEC is formed • US Food and Drug Administration approves birth control pill • John F Kennedy is elected US President	1960	• National institutions are formed in the 1960s: Housing & Development Board, Economic Development Board, People's Association • Formation of Malaysia is proposed by Tungku Abdul Rahman
Bay of Pigs Invasion (of Cuba)	1961	• Women's Charter is passed • Bukit Ho Swee Fire • Barisan Sosialis breaks from PAP
Cuban missile crisis	1962	
• Martin Luther King's "I have a dream" speech • John F Kennedy is assassinated • Lyndon B Johnson is sworn in as US President	1963	• Operation Coldstore follows the industrial & political unrest of the 1950s • Merger to form Malaysia • Indonesian President Sukarno launches Confrontation policy • Black & White TV comes to Singapore
• Vietnam War intensifies • Nelson Mandela is given life imprisonment	1964	Prophet Muhammad's birthday racial riots
• Ferdinand Marcos becomes Philippines President • 1st spacewalk by man	1965	Separation from Malaysia: Independence
• Indira Gandhi becomes Indian Prime Minister • Cultural Revolution in China	1966	• 1st disco in town opens • Bilingual policy is introduced in schools • Family Planning and Population Board is formed
• Riots in Hong Kong • ASEAN is formed	1967	National Service is instituted

(Continued)

Table 2: (*Continued*)

World Events	Year	Events Relevant to Singapore
• Martin Luther King, Robert Kennedy are assassinated • Richard Nixon is elected US President • Student movement spreads to Europe	1968	• Britain announces early withdrawal of troops from Singapore • General Election: PAP wins all seats
• Neil Armstrong walks on the moon • Concorde's first flight	1969	May 13 racial riot
Prince Sihanouk is ousted in Cambodia	1970	Tun Abdul Razak succeeds Tunku Abdul Rahman as Malaysian Prime Minister
Bangladesh becomes independent	1971	
Richard Nixon visits China, thaw in Cold War	1972	• National Wages Council is set up • General Election: PAP wins all seats
• Watergate scandal • Yom Kippur War • Arab oil embargo • Energy crisis	1973	Recession results from rise in international oil price
	1974	• Newspaper & Printing Presses Act is passed • Colour TV comes to Singapore
• Chiang Kai Shek dies • Saigon falls, start of Vietnamese boat people	1975	
• Zhou Enlai, Mao Tse Tung die • Jimmy Carter is elected US President	1976	• Continued internal communist unrest • General Election: PAP wins all seats
Deng Xiaoping is restored to power	1977	
Vietnam invades Cambodia	1978	Deng Xiaoping visits Singapore

(*Continued*)

Table 2: (*Continued*)

World Events	Year	Events Relevant to Singapore
• US & China reach full diplomatic relations • Shah of Iran is exiled • China invades North Vietnam • Margaret Thatcher is elected UK Prime Minister • USSR invades Afghanistan	1979	• Courtesy and Speak Mandarin campaigns are launched • SSO debuts • 1st McDonald's outlet • Pop culture of late 70s — Kungfu films, *The Godfather*, *Star Wars*, Michael Jackson
• Iran–Iraq War (till 1988) • Ronald Reagan is elected US President	1980	• Nantah merges with University of Singapore • General Election: PAP wins all seats
• Mahathir Mohamed becomes Malaysian Prime Minister • 1st AIDS case is diagnosed • IBM introduces the PC	1981	• Changi Airport opens • J B Jeyaretnam wins Anson by-election
• Philips invents the CD • Time Magazine nominates the computer as "Man of the Year"	1982	
Microsoft releases Word	1983	
Apple introduces Macintosh	1984	

We have arrived at Generation X. Their formative years were from the early 1980s to the mid-1990s.

Table 3: Signposts for Generation X (born 1965–1980), in Singapore and the world, based on Lim, *Chronicles of Singapore, 1959 to 2009*.

World Events	Year	Events Relevant to Singapore
HIV is discovered	1983	
Indira Gandhi is assassinated	1984	• General Election: PAP vote slides • Three women MPs are elected
• People Power • Corazon Aquino is elected Philippines President • Mad Cow Disease is discovered	1986	PAP Youth Wing is formed

(Continued)

Table 3: *(Continued)*

World Events	Year	Events Relevant to Singapore
Black Monday stock market crash	1987	• Marxist plot arrests • Reversal of population policy to three children • MRT starts rolling
Benazir Bhutto becomes Pakistan's Prime Minister	1988	• General Election: GRCs are adopted • PAP wins 80/81 seats • First NCMPs are appointed
• Tiananmen Square massacre • Fall of Berlin Wall	1989	• National Ideology/ Shared Values is introduced • PAP Women's Wing is formed • Pop culture: more vibe, sports, art & culture promoted • National Day street parties • Art censorship becomes more liberal
• East & West Germany are united • Iraq invades Kuwait • Gulf War	1990	• NMPs are sworn in • Goh Chok Tong becomes Singapore's second Prime Minister
	1991	• The Next Lap is published • General Election: PAP wins 77/81 seats
• Serbia besieges Bosnia–Herzegovina • Recession	1992	Marine Parade by-election
• EU is formed • Bill Clinton is elected (1st Baby Boomer President)	1993	Ong Teng Cheong becomes 1st elected President
• Nelson Mandela is elected South Africa's President • Kim Jong Il becomes North Korea's President	1994	• White Paper on Competitive Salaries for Competent & Honest Government is released • SingTel launches SingNet (internet service)

(Continued)

Table 3: (*Continued*)

World Events	Year	Events Relevant to Singapore
	1995	Cable TV comes to Singapore
• Creutzfeldt-Jakobson variant of Mad Cow Disease is discovered • Dolly the sheep is cloned	1996	

For Generation Y, the teen years were in the mid-1990s and up to 2010. The significant world events would be the rise of China, Hong Kong reverting back to China, and then, in 1997, the Asian Financial Crisis and the bird flu pandemic. At home we suffered the haze; we had a SilkAir crash. In 1998, Suharto resigned and there were race riots against the Chinese in Jakarta. The world financial crisis 2007–2008 hit us; fortunately we recovered from it quite speedily.

Table 4: Signposts for Generation Y (born 1981–1995), in Singapore and the world, based on Lim, *Chronicles of Singapore, 1959 to 2009.*

World Events	Year	Events Relevant to Singapore
• Tony Blair is elected UK Prime Minister • Hong Kong reverts to China • Asian financial crisis • Bird flu pandemic	1997	• General Election: PAP wins 81/83 seats • Haze becomes a problem for the first time • SilkAir crash
• Suharto resigns • Rioting against Chinese businesses in Jakarta	1998	• Asian financial crisis forces cost-cutting measures • Singapore team climbs Mt Everest
	1999	S21 Report (inclusive society)
• Chen Shui-Bian is elected President, ROC • Vladimir Putin becomes President of Russia • George W Bush is elected US President	2000	• Speakers' Corner set up • Expedition to Antarctica • First NEWater production plant opens

(*Continued*)

Table 4: (*Continued*)

World Events	Year	Events Relevant to Singapore
• Gloria Arroyo is elected Philippines President • Thaksin Shinawat is elected Prime Minister of Thailand • Megawati is elected President of Indonesia • September 11 terrorist attack, World Trade Centre	2001	• General Election: PAP wins 82/84 seats • Jemaah Islamiyah (JI) terrorist cell/plot is uncovered, arrests are made
• Dotcom bust reaches bottom • Bali terrorist bombings	2002	• Further JI arrests • Esplanade Theatres opens
• SARS outbreak • Saddam Hussein is captured • Abdullah Badawi succeeds Mahathir Mohamad	2003	• SARS in Singapore • Declaration on Religious Harmony • Goh Chok Tong announces civil service will accept gay employees
• Susilo Bambang Yudhoyono is elected President of Indonesia • Asian tsunami kills over 225,000	2004	• Lee Hsien Loong becomes Prime Minister • Sports School is announced
	2005	Two casinos are announced
Thaksin Shinawat is deposed in a coup	2006	• Bad haze is back • General Election: PAP wins 82/84 seats
• Gordon Brown becomes UK Prime Minister • Kevin Rudd becomes Australian Prime Minister • Benazir Bhutto is assassinated	2007	*2007–2008*: World financial crisis
• Fidel Castro steps down • China suppresses protests by Tibetan monks • Sichuan earthquake • Beijing Olympics • Collapse of Lehman Brothers • Barack Obama is elected US President • Terrorist attack in Mumbai • Cyclone Nargis in Myanmar	2008	• Government dips into reserves for the first time • Remaking of Heartland: Waterfront Town (PM's National Day Rally 2007) • Singapore gets a silver medal at Beijing Olympics • F1 comes to town

(*Continued*)

Table 4: (*Continued*)

World Events	Year	Events Relevant to Singapore
Sri Lanka civil war ends	2009	• H1N1 alert • Mas Selamat is recaptured • Population increases to 4.8m (with 1.2m foreigners) • PM's Nation Day Rally – Singapore's challenges: Economic uncertainty, Ageing population, Healthcare • AWARE saga
	2010	• PM's National Day Rally: Foreigners, HDB prices, Education • Integrated Resorts open • Youth Olympic Games

The September 11 (2001) terrorist attack at the World Trade Centre was a defining moment for all the peoples around the world, including Singaporeans. Life has never remained the same again after that. Generation Y is living in a world full of uncertainties, with all kinds of threats to life and liberty, such as the SARS outbreak in 2003.

What do the events recorded in these tables mean? How do we read the tea leaves, so to speak? What is there to say about the generations in Singapore?

The Traditionals, my generation, grew up during the colonial era. They went through World War II and the Japanese Occupation. There were economic hardships, but they retained old virtues, hard work, thriftiness and so on. The family was upheld. The Chinese among the Singapore population were caught up in the surge of Chinese nationalism and communist ideals in the early 1960s. They were drawn later into Singapore's independence struggle.

The Baby Boomers grew up in turbulent times. There were law and order problems, unemployment, communist and communalist strife, merger and separation. However, they also experienced improvements to their livelihood. They went through recession, but later they were the beneficiaries of the prosperity of the 1990s, the decade of uninterrupted prosperity. Generally staunch supporters of the PAP, they were involved in building up a hard-working, honest, united nation, but they led a clean and relatively dull life. They were beginning to be exposed to western culture. To them, money was the symbol of competitive success.

Generation X, my children's generation, lived through Singapore's economic restructuring. From low-skill, low-wage to high-wage economy. Generation X is what is often referred to as the post-independence generation. They witnessed economic prosperity and double-digit growth. They had many years of stability and security. Women received equal education opportunities; they worked outside the home; families became smaller; divorce was on the rise (similar to the social changes happening to Generation X in the West). In Singapore, there was the growth of opposition politics after the 1981 Anson by-election. The political system slowly opened up and Goh Chok Tong promised a kinder, gentler type of government.

This generation lived with the computer. They had to learn and they learnt very fast. But they were not born with the computer, unlike Generation Y. Alongside the use of computers and the growth of the internet, there was an opening up of the arts and sports scene. There was an atmosphere of less censorship, more individual growth. But what were their values and work ethics? Generation X teenagers grew up being called job-hoppers. Job-hopping during economic prosperity was very common.

Generation Y in Singapore

Generation Y is the current generation, which first entered work in the last 10–15 years. This generation started when Singapore entered the global knowledge economy. But their world is full of uncertainty. There are the viruses, bird flu, H1N1, variants of mad cow disease, things that cannot be tamed by antibiotics. Then there are environmental and ethical issues — things like cloning technology, natural disasters, and also the threat of terrorism. On top of that they went through a world financial crisis, and some in the financial sector who earned a lot of money have lost their jobs because of it.

The society of this generation promises to be more inclusive with Lee Hsien Loong becoming the PM. And they are at a crossroads in the battle for talent. They are globally oriented. They have to compete with foreigners; there is widening income inequality. They grew up with the internet and I think they value creativity more than entrepreneurship. There are some data which show this. However, I think young Singaporeans are beginning to change. They want to be their own boss. They don't want to work in government service, not so much as before, not being so much in need of job security. They want to venture out into the world. They are adventurous in their travels, in taste, and they emphasise lifestyle choices.

Now, what are the Generation Y values and work ethics? The previous Singapore generations, Generation X, the Baby Boomers, especially the Traditionals, all these were not so similar to the corresponding western generations of the same name. But for Generation Y, there seems to be a convergence between the Singapore and the western counterparts.

I saw a report of a study by the Singapore Human Resource Institute, done in 2008, on the generation who were aged between 15 and 31.[6] The characteristics of the Generation Y were reported there as confident, tech-savvy, unconventional, restless. They are unable to concentrate on one particular thing for long. Of those surveyed, 27% had not identified their profession of choice. These are 15- to 31-year-olds. They job-hop, they switch careers and 71% agreed that this is a norm. They have three big top expenditures: alcohol and wine; mobile phones; and food. In short, lifestyle. They like to travel, backpacking to see the world and they also like to take mid-career sabbaticals. Finding self is a big thing for them.

---

[6] Sandra Leong, "Understanding Y". *Sunday Times*, 26 September 2010, 6–7.

Are the younger generations sufficiently prepared for the possibilities of hardships or contractions in the future? You look at the size of India, China, South America, there is going to be a resource problem globally and we are going to have to face this.

The implication of your question is that they are not well prepared. But if you look at the recent [2008] financial crisis, the number of people who lost their jobs, who were in the middle management, executives, I think they went through quite a lot. This thing really hit us hard, although we were somewhat cushioned by the government's measures. But parents who have lost their jobs are bound to affect their families and the teenagers growing up with them. Depending on the seriousness of the family hardships, some young people would have known hardship through the family.

A second thing is that we have been increasingly encouraging people to go overseas for attachments or exchanges. These are very educational and very beneficial to the young people, and if they have participated in some humanitarian projects, even better. So I think our young people can be exposed to the hardships — and nothing can compare to actually doing things with your hands and seeing for yourselves — not just reading about issues like world poverty. Poverty, depression, drugs, abuse, negligence. These seem to be issues elsewhere. Our children are much less exposed to these kinds of situations, and I think they are very lucky. So you need to expose them to the world.

— From the Question & Answer session

Illustrating this last point, a 24-year-old woman was quoted as saying, "I am lucky because I am young. I have no commitments. So, I can take my time to find myself and decide on the direction I want my life to go in." It's a very privileged generation who are free to make a choice like that, and say it. But this generation also has to fend for itself, face foreign competition, face the global world and a new century of great uncertainties.

The National Youth Council carries out national surveys regularly. In 2002 they did one, and in 2005, they did another. Now, in 2010, they have just completed one more. Nationally representative samples like these, of over 1,500 people aged 15 to 29, show you the trend much more accurately.[7]

> **I belong to Gen Y. Yes, I question authority at work. I take mid-life sabbaticals to find myself. But having said that, could you elaborate on the "straddle generation"? Because I was born in 1981, I suppose I would have some influences from the values of Gen X.**
>
> These are rather arbitrary divisions, though every generation does happen to correspond with a different phase in Singapore's development. But history is a continuous flow and people are very selective in what they think is relevant. In a globalised world you cannot afford to isolate yourself from what is happening in the rest of the world. In the case of Americans, it has been said that they used to be very parochial, just knowing about their own local states, politics and so on. But they were large enough to be able to do that. Singapore is so small. Here we have to be globally orientated; you cannot afford to shut off the world. So young people must form the habit of following the news, must be alert and informed. Otherwise we will be adrift and so affected that we will not be able to have a firm core and be able to take on the world. So we need to straddle generations.
>
> — *From the Question & Answer session*

---

[7] Ho Kong Chong and Wynne Chia, *Youth.sg: The State of Youth in Singapore 2006*, 2nd Edition. (Singapore: National Youth Council, 2006). For the 2010 Survey results, please see *Youth Statistics in Brief 2013* (Singapore: National Youth Council, 2013). The Brief contains comparisons between the 2005 and 2010 findings on youths' values and attitudes.

These surveys show that the life goals of young people between 2002 and 2005 are quite similar. The most important thing to them is still education and learning; they want new skills and knowledge, followed by earning lots of money. Then, only third is getting married. Other things are not so important. However, between 2002 and 2005 there was quite an increase in people who said they wanted to be active in sports, probably as a result of our promotion of sports and a more active healthy lifestyle. In both cohorts, Y and Z, the importance of "having fame" is low.

There were more interesting findings. When they are worried and troubled, who is the first person they would turn to, these young 15- to 29-year-olds? Their mother. As they grow older, they turn to her less; they more consistently turn to friends.[8] The father is insignificant. And unfortunately, the siblings are also not playing much role either. This generation, even though they may have siblings at home, may not communicate with each other or share very much with each other.

Comparing views on marriage, we have a world youth survey,[9] and can compare views across countries. Korea, Japan and Singapore are roughly similar in terms of people who answer "very important" or "quite important" to the questions on this topic. When the question asked is about whether one should marry, in Germany and Sweden there is a majority saying that it is better not to marry, or not necessary to marry; but a clear majority in the three Asian countries say one should get married, or that it is better to get married. The United States has a bare majority in this direction. But on divorce, Korea, Japan and Singapore differ. In Japan, I was surprised to learn that 37.5% say you can divorce regardless of whether you have children or not. Whereas in Singapore and Korea over 50% think that you should not divorce, or only if you have no children. In Germany and Sweden, and also the United States, the view is that you should divorce if there is no love, or no children.

---

[8] The survey did not ask specifically about boyfriends, girlfriends or spouses as sources of support (for older respondents), but these may have been important too.

[9] In Ho and Chia, already cited.

We can also look at values in the 2002 and 2005 National Youth Surveys mentioned. Friends, families, and work are all important, as is leisure. Religion is somewhat less important, politics less still, though both religion and leisure rate slightly more important in 2005 than in 2002; however, these are small effects in the general profile of values.

Is the convergence of Gen Y here with Gen Y in the United States a global phenomenon, and will we see more of it with Gen Z?

Singapore now belongs to the so-called first world of developed countries, and young people's mentalities are bound to be quite comparable with other such societies. But much of the world is still not first world. And here in Singapore, some of our fundamental values are still Asian. Over the years you see some weakening of the emphasis on things like filial piety, respect and care for the elderly. But young people on the other hand are also compassionate; they are much more sympathetic to the issues faced by the disabled, the disadvantaged and they care about the world.

So what does this mean in terms of intergeneration relations? The social contract is changing. Older citizens are capable of being independent and they have to accept the younger ones' change in orientation to different issues. Older folks should make themselves useful; younger ones should appreciate them, and not take them for granted, because the young will grow old too.

— From the Question & Answer session

Finally, here are some questions to reflect on regarding the challenges facing youth today.

Challenges in education. As formal education lengthens, lifelong learning is required. Singapore has recognised this and aims to promote it very actively. This increasing importance of education for success in life reflects the increased range of educational choices and pathways now as compared to 10 or 15 years ago; but there remains intense competition for academic achievement.

The work that young people face. The challenges arise because we now have a knowledge-based economy. This needs creativity and innovation. At work, you have people from different cultures and nationalities. The workforce is much more diverse. Employment is globalised and very competitive. The current management practice of outsourcing, providing contract work rather than permanent employment, increases job instability. But there is increasing work overseas and frequent travel.

The family. Challenges arise from the increase in the female labour force participation, with later marriage and smaller families. There are now smaller extended family networks for social support, divorce rates are rising and single-headed households more common. And as a result, there are emerging issues around how bonding can be sustained across generations.

Challenges in the community. In the community today, there are multiple group affiliations, which can be local or foreign. They can be virtual online affiliations, or actual physical communities. But there is a corresponding decline in traditional community networks and associations. Young people nowadays have wide networks, but I think most of the ties in that network are rather weak.

Lifestyle challenges. A consumer-oriented lifestyle, and the rising importance of leisure, art and sports, reflect the demand of younger people for lifestyle choices. Integrated resorts and the Singapore F1 night races illustrate the globalisation of leisure and affluence. Yet I think our youth also aspire to active citizenry, and many are concerned with environmental and conservation issues.

And so, trying to make sense of the generations, trying to see where our youth are heading, and understanding them and those who went before them, reveals the challenges facing young people today.

CHAPTER FIVE

Preparing Our Children for the World of Tomorrow

Ho Kwon Ping

About the Speaker

Mr Ho Kwon Ping is Executive Chairman of Banyan Tree Holdings, which owns both listed and private companies engaged in the development, ownership and operation of hotels, resorts, spas, residential homes, retail galleries and other lifestyle activities around the world. Born in 1952, he was educated in Tunghai University, Taiwan, followed by Stanford University, California and the University of Singapore. After a career in broadcasting and financial journalism, when he was the Economics Editor of the *Far Eastern Economic Review*, he is today Chairman of Singapore Management University.

However, he is far from the conventional stereotype of a corporate executive, or a university chairman. This is a man who in his youth was briefly detained under the Internal Security Act, and was once a young backpacker in rural Southeast Asia, filled with enthusiasm for revolutionary ideals. Even in 2011, as a mature CEO, he was nonetheless mindful of the legacy of Che Guevara when he visited South America. Yet, he recently described the political pioneers of Singapore as possessing pragmatic genius.

Mr Ho became the first Asian to receive the American Creativity Association Lifetime Achievement Award in recognition of his creativity and innovation in various spheres of endeavour, and in 2011 — the year of the lecture recorded in this book — he was voted Top Thinker in Singapore in the Yahoo! Singapore 9 Awards, a testament to his business innovations and leadership in civic causes. He holds the London Business School 2005 Entrepreneurship Award. In 2008, he was named CEO of the Year at the Singapore Corporate Awards. He also holds the Singapore Government Meritorious Service Medal for his contribution in the founding of SMU, and an honorary doctorate from Johnson & Wales University, Rhode Island. Mr Ho is married to Claire Chiang, Senior Vice President, Banyan Tree Holdings Ltd. They have two sons and a daughter.

Mr Ho therefore approached the Children's Society 5th Lecture as a parent and with great experience in the University of Life, but with some diffidence. When first invited he remarked that "this is out of my area of expertise. I really am not sure what I'm going to say." In fact, his lecture had the greatest possible relevance for parents, as he addressed issues of the importance of family values and of practical and intellectual self-reliance, in the raising of children.

Reflecting three years after his lecture, Mr Ho made clear his commitment to a more equalitarian society. He raised doubts about the perpetuation of elitism and social stratification — not to be confused with the encouragement and recognition of excellence — and the many paths by which it can be reached. He expressed reservations about the commitment to academic excellence as almost the sole kind of recognised excellence — what he calls the Mandarin tradition — because it fails to give recognition to excellence in other areas of life and work, including those usually regarded as "blue-collar". He saw social stratification as a risk of the Gifted Education Programme.

Ho Kwon Ping as a boy

Ho Kwon Ping also reiterated the importance, in his view, of having children speak for themselves and hearing their voices — a view very consistent with the UN Convention on the Rights of the Child, to which Singapore is a signatory, and which it has ratified. He felt that children often had a unique if naïve curiosity, and passionately reasserted the importance of encouraging and answering children who ask "why?" He was clear that values are key and are "caught not taught", that is, they are acquired by example and not by instruction; or at least, that where instruction and example diverge, it is the example that will be followed.

The 5th Lecture, delivered 22 October 2011

Today is the first time I've been asked to talk about children as such. I must say this is certainly an area that is totally beyond my expertise. But I was told, "Never mind. That's what all the other speakers have said. Nobody is an expert on children. But if you're a father, then you always think you're an expert." And so, since I am a father, then I suppose I will call myself an expert.

I must also admit that I did not know much about the Children's Society before I was invited to give this talk. But the more that I learnt about it, the more impressed I was with the work that the Children's Society has done. I think that we in Banyan Tree, like many of you, who place children at the heart of society's problems as well as its progress, also believe in the primacy of children. And one of our keystone programmes is called Seedlings, because, obviously, we are a tree. It's a programme where each of our hotels around the world select young people at risk, just as you are also dedicated to serving the needs of children at risk. We mentor youngsters who are at risk, and we give them after-school work in various departments of our hotels until they reach an age when we either can hire them, or we can let them go into the world with employable skills. But my talk today isn't really about children at risk or in need. I'd like to speak on a broader topic, namely "How can we prepare our children for the world of tomorrow?"

Now, the quick and easy answer of course is simply education and Singapore does it, I must say quite unequivocally, extremely well. And although as parents we all have criticisms of our own schools, and are arguably even more critical than outside observers, we all know that education has always been at the forefront of Singapore's strategy for survival and for prosperity. Our literacy and our numeracy achievements are studied by other countries. And I think with a national state-supervised system, we do have a system that's arguably able to deliver good education to most students — and not an excellent education to an elite few through private schools, with mediocre schooling to the rest through relatively bad state schools. That is the situation in most other countries such as America or even the UK, where we read about peaks of excellence through fantastic universities and boarding schools, but which are all very expensive private schools. And they are contrasted with national systems which are really as antiquated as the physical infrastructure of most of those countries. So for a system which has got to be totally national, we do have a pretty good system.

Moreover, our schools, from primary to tertiary, are indeed gearing up for the world of tomorrow. Having spent the last few decades basically imparting skills and knowledge for our young to succeed in this economy, our schools are now gearing students to learn how to think, rather than just to remember facts. And all this talk about a knowledge-based economy is of course backed by an educational system which is more flexible than before. I say this not with expertise, but with conviction, because, as a person who hasn't really studied in the Singapore educational system, I have always been, throughout my life, one of the most vociferous critics of this system, as being a very dehumanising and mechanical system. Of course I was very surprised, when, as a big critic of the system, I was then asked to head up Singapore Management University (SMU). But this is the government strategy — you co-opt your critics.

However, I must say they gave me a lot of leeway. And my years with SMU since 2000 have convinced me, with the pedagogy we are allowed to maintain in SMU and the students that we have produced, that our students are indeed able to be as problem-solving, creative and analytical as the best students from other developed countries. I am quite gratified that having delivered basic learning skills, our educational system is now embarking on what our Minister for Education recently called "a student-centric values-driven education". This new character and citizenship curriculum, with its own dedicated Continuing Education branch to implement it, is of course, by itself, encouraging news. The danger is that values cannot be imparted only by formal syllabuses, and the bureaucratisation of character building can quite easily backfire.

When I read in the newspaper that values such as integrity, respect, patriotism, are all going to be taught in the new curriculum, I began to get a bit more concerned. I hope that this new curriculum will not be simply a repackaging, a version of the old civics and moral education classes of the past, jazzed up with computer animation and so on. No matter how engaging or interactive the pedagogy, if the new courses are going to be simply top-down lectures or even project work with a fixed curriculum, I think the impact on our young will be limited. Values, I believe, are absorbed through personal experience, not through academic pedagogy alone.

Is project work the answer?

Project work is more part of the curriculum than individual homework, but that is just one example. I would prefer to think more about the reliance on grades for secondary and primary schools. There is no reason why you cannot have a more balanced scorecard method of ranking students. For example I, for one, do believe, as in American education, that sport is very important — not for physical prowess, but because in sports you learn a lot of self-discipline, you learn team work, you learn how to cope with disappointments. Early on in life, sport is a way by which you can learn a lot about yourself. And I think in that sense, if we develop a balanced scorecard for measuring a child, so that it's not just grades alone, and if we apply that through schools, then we will have the better schools accepting students who are not purely graded by academic excellence, but through a balanced scorecard of achievements.

— From the Question & Answer session

The concept of experiential learning is probably the most powerful way to impart values to young people. That is why, instead of just ethics courses in SMU itself, we ensure that every student in

SMU must undergo a certain number of hours of community service before graduation. We believe that at the heart of ethical values is a sense of responsibility to the community and young people acquire this sensibility through doing, through interacting with the old, the poor, the disabled, the disadvantaged rather than just watching about such things through video films or lectures by professors.

And therefore this means not designing an academic character and citizenship curriculum as such, but designing opportunities where character is tested and forged, such as in sports, or where values are created through provocative discussions. There is a whole field called situational ethics where people are presented with, or share, ethical predicaments in their lives and they then discuss these dilemmas. The premise is that there is no black and white to ethics, and that much of ethics is situational, and if we are going to live ethical lives, we must confront such dilemmas and learn how we would actually deal with them. And as I have said above, values are imparted through learning opportunities, which more often than not are outside the classroom. If our educational system is going to impart values, I believe it has to take a holistic approach and understand that leadership, values and integrity should be taught in a holistic and situated manner.

Nevertheless, I'm not even here to talk about education. No matter how enlightened, education can only go so far in preparing our children for the world of tomorrow. Education can prepare them with all the skill sets for specific tasks, but not with the fortitude, the resilience, the values and the ideals, which can take them through external challenges as well as internal self-doubt. Such doubts will clearly plague our young as they live their lives, just as internal self-doubts have plagued us all at times throughout our own lives. These values and attributes of fortitude and resilience can only be imparted by family, friends and individual inspirational mentors, whether a teacher, a parent, a sibling or a relative. And so, in short, the task of preparing our children for the future must lie with the community at large, and not just with the school itself.

How do you impart these values within an educational system that only seems to promote more skills for people to succeed in the new economy?

My own experience is that it can be done. People used to say that Singapore students were not very articulate, couldn't really think fast on their feet, couldn't compare to the foreign students and were only very mechanical thinkers, very good with grades; but I think with SMU we have proven that this is not the case. The students are typical young Singaporeans, but we teach them to think for themselves. We force them to think for themselves. There is a debate about what you have to do to make people think for themselves. But the critical point is, once you acknowledge that the purpose of education is teaching people to think — not teaching people what to think, but basically how to think — then there's a whole sea change in methodology. And the Ministry of Education seems to think we should go in that direction.

— From the Question & Answer session

I've never put much credence into relying on what I would say, to put it quite politely, my rather colourful foray into tertiary education. I think my CV mentions that I went to three universities. It does not mention that though I attended three universities in three countries, I only graduated from one, was kicked out from another, and took nine years to get a basic bachelor's degree. And of course the irony is I'm now heading up a university. So, as a result of that, I think I bring a relatively cynical and frank view about the need to not rely too much on schools and education. And certainly, it has never been the basis of whatever modest success that I have achieved so far. But whatever mixed success I might have achieved in my life, which I do not attribute to formal education, least of all my academically mediocre succession of primary and secondary schools in Thailand, can perhaps be attributed to the values and attitudes which my parents imbued in me from young.

For example, a very strong social conscience. My father came from a poor background, my mother from a wealthy one. But both of them harboured, since their student days, a keen sense of the injustices of colonialism. They were both student activists in China. And much later, as parents generally, and at dinner table conversations, they imparted their own values of social responsibility through stories about their own youth. And perhaps, even more than that, they imparted to me, and taught me the need to always question everything, even what they themselves taught me, until I could only accept a truth which I discovered through my own reasoning, rather than by simple acceptance of common norms and rules.

How do parents and families impart values, given the way that society is being structured today?

I think that's a very deep dilemma. If you look at some of the northern European countries, in Scandinavia for example, I think they have come to realise that we may have to sacrifice economic growth to some extent, for a more balanced society. We may have to allow mothers, and fathers of course, to spend more time at home with the children in their early years. We cannot have a society go on where essentially we outsource everything to providers so that the "economic digits" in society can just do what they are best doing, which is creating wealth. Something has to give. To me, we do have to consider a trade-off.

I know it's not fair but a lot of women, professional women, have considered the trade-off. In a fairer society, perhaps, the husband would take off a few years from work to help raise the children. That is the kind of trade-off that a couple may have to decide. Because if you are going to have maids to impart values to the children, that is really abdicating a fundamental parental role. You do have to have maids in a society where both parents are working. But even the dependence on maids, I suppose, can be re-thought to some extent. As far as grandparents are concerned, we have to look at other issues. A lot of societies are looking at how housing can be developed in such a way that you can have multigenerational living so that people do not have to be so far away from each other. Complex social issues are involved in this, but I don't think we can run away from it.

The very heart of all these policy issues is that central question: How are we going to prepare our children for tomorrow? Does it start with imparting values from the family? If that is the case, then a lot of other social issues dealing with employment of maids, dealing with teaching, dealing with housing and so on, all have to be considered.

The fundamental issue must be: Do we agree that values must be imparted primarily and fundamentally at home? If we think we can basically outsource this to schools and maids, then a totally different set of considerations apply.

— *From the Question & Answer session*

This lesson that they imparted to me, I've tried to impart to others. Not long ago I gave a talk to my youngest son's secondary school, and being a secondary school, I had to make it more interesting so I started by asking them what is the most liberating and at the same time most dangerous three-letter word in the English language. And I suggested that for boys with raging hormones, the word is invariably s-e-x. And for the pious (this was a mission school) invariably the most liberating three letter word would be God. But it was a great disappointment to them that I didn't agree that sex was the most liberating word. Because for me, truly, the most liberating, and at the same time most dangerous three letter word, is "why".

By asking "why?" of everything around you, you develop a keenly inquisitive intellect and an attitude of critical enquiry. That liberates the mind to explore so many things that you would not have explored before, and to discover things for yourself and truths for yourself. At the same time, it can also be dangerous. Asking "why?" got me into enormous trouble with my teachers, who, I remember, always just told me to shut up and sit down. Asking "why?" also led me to being thrown out of university. Asking "why?" also led me to spend two months in jail in Singapore under the Internal Security Act.

But it also has been liberating, and not only to me. If you look around, asking "why?" was the reason the greatest scientists discovered unknown truths of the universe, or doctors conquered incurable diseases, or social activists liberated entire societies or races from colonial oppression or racial apartheid. So if I have to be simplistic and choose one thing to impart to the children of tomorrow, it is to have them continue to ask "why?" of the world around them, and to persist in asking until they have found answers which are to their own satisfaction.

The ability to ask "why?" will lead us to become leaders in the life sciences and creative industries which will power our economy in the future. It will lead us to new social and political norms, of which the recent elections [2011] have already given us an inkling. It will enable us to confront yet unknown challenges and dilemmas with the fierce determination to keep asking until we get the answers.

Now, how do we as a society inculcate this WHY attitude amongst our young? I think it all begins, of course, at the family level, where values and attitudes are first learnt. As any parent will testify, children in their innocence can ask incredibly penetrating questions which are often embarrassing for adults to answer. And so, therefore, the first lesson for all young parents today is: do not shut children up, do not treat them as ignorant, do not stifle the inherent curiosity and honesty of the young, and instead, take their innocence as a virtue which can be honed into a continually engaging mind.

At the school level, teachers can channel that WHY attitude, if it's been developed at home, into a search for answers and a thirst for knowledge which will accompany children into adulthood. At the corporate level, bosses can encourage subordinates to speak their mind, to offer out-of-the-box ideas and to take initiatives. And at the societal level, our community can tolerate and even celebrate failure if the effort has been noble.

As I look back at how my wife and I brought up our children, I can think of a few specific things which my wife and I did to prepare our children with the values which will arm them for life's challenges. At first, from young, we prepared them to understand the importance and the tradition of family. Our children always spend one dinner a week with my parents, their grandparents, alone, without my wife and I, so that they could interact and value each other more profoundly, and understand tradition, and understand age and the relativity between youth and age, and learn from them.

We prepared our children to be independent. When my eldest son reached 18 years of age, I gave him just a few hundred dollars and I asked him to take a plane to Hanoi by himself and spend a week there on his own without any friend or any plan. He did it and he was very happy and I think it's opened him up to the fact that you can be, from very young, an independent person. Since then, his younger sister has done even crazier things. She's gone skydiving by herself without permission from her parents. She's gone climbing Mount Fuji on her own. And I don't even dare to think of what my youngest son will do when he's reached 18, and is supposed to go out and do something on his own.

On attitudes, values and good behaviour

Children are not clones of their parents. They should have their own attitudes. When I refer to values, I think values must be imparted to children, but it's not as if they should be clones where attitudes are concerned. I don't think that if your parents had a lower risk-taking attitude, then you should have a lower risk-taking attitude, etc. We are all products of our own environment and there is also free will to be considered. But in terms of attitude in a different sense, not about risk-taking, but about respect for people and so on, in my family we are totally illiberal. We do not and will not tolerate impoliteness by our children to other people. We will not tolerate lack of respect. We are not like a lot of American families; we are very, very disciplined in that respect. You do not talk back to your elders, you do not talk back to other people, and so on. So on one hand we made it very clear that deep down they should have a sceptical attitude about everything, but on the other hand, they cannot exhibit behaviour which is anti-social and disrespectful of other people. So I just want to clarify that, when one wants to develop in people an attitude of critical enquiry and asking "why?", it doesn't mean that you should tolerate your children then becoming disrespectful to you.

— From the Question & Answer session

We prepared our children to think for themselves. My wife and I have always insisted on dinner table conversations, where our children are challenged to think for themselves, and to ask difficult questions and to defend their own positions. And sometimes when our children's friends come home for dinner, they really think we're having a huge fight at home because it's like a debate where everybody is talking at the same time. Because if you do not learn how to speak up, then you won't survive at our dinner table. And it trained them to be independent. Of course our youngest son is the smartest one. While the rest of us fight, he's just basically eating all the rest of the food.

We also taught our children to be committed life partners. My wife and I allow our own relationship between ourselves to unveil itself in an unalloyed fashion so that our children can see us whether we are very affectionate, or nagging each other or even having arguments. We then use these learning moments to teach our children what married life will eventually be like, so that they can be better wives and husbands. And as we know, a lot of children who come from broken homes themselves do not end up with happy marriages. So it is very important to create an environment at home which your children can subtly learn from, and put into practice when they have their own life partners.

And so for my wife and I, every event has been a learning opportunity. Not to pontificate, but to continually and gently guide our children to understand important lessons, which have become, I hope, part of their life values. Of course I say this from a somewhat jaundiced perspective. My children, if they were here today, would probably not agree with you that it was that gentle and wise. But the advantage of age is you get to say what you want to say and other people have to listen to you.

How do you teach children values when you are wealthy?

I think that's a good question because I see this problem when I go to China; I see it everywhere around me. As Asia becomes wealthier and wealthier, too many children are spoilt by their parents; it's a very *nouveau riche* phenomenon. Families in Europe which have been rich for generations make a better job of teaching children how to be humble and frugal in life, because in that culture they have learned that those who didn't basically lost their family money very early on.

In my own case, my children had allowances that were less than what their counterparts in school enjoyed. They had to learn that the family wealth doesn't belong to them, and that they are custodians of that wealth for the next generation, and that's all they are. They had the occasional indulgence, like anybody. But now, they have no branded clothes, they themselves buy second-hand cars, and after a while, we realised that frugal values have become part of their own values and frankly, if we gave our children a few million dollars in cash, they would just put it away in the bank. I think this is the kind of lesson that all of us as parents have to teach our children from young. Your children are probably going to become wealthier than they need to be, and from an early age they need to learn values of frugality, and, also very importantly, not to get caught in that rat race of showing off to other kids.

I think this is an important lesson because you will probably find as parents that your kids are going to compare more and say *so-and-so has this, so-and-so has that, and how come I don't have*, and they feel that you are not giving them the right things, or they even feel shy if they own an older iPhone than their friend who owns a newer iPhone, and so on. These are excellent teaching moments. There are so many teaching moments in a parent–child relationship where you can use an example like that and teach them the value of frugality, teach them the value of self-respect, not to care what other people think about you, it only matters what you think about yourself. So throughout your entire interaction with your child, there are so many opportunities to impart values, and it's not sitting them down and giving them a lecture on "values" with a capital "V".

— From the Question & Answer session

I think all of us know at the very end the painful truth, and that is that no matter how hard we try, we can never fully prepare our children for tomorrow. But we can comfort ourselves that if we try hard enough, though we may not be able to provide answers to their questions, we can, by asking the right questions, help to point them towards finding their own solutions.

And so to all of you in the Children's Society and other organisations who have taken upon yourselves the deeply gratifying, the hugely responsible and the tremendously challenging task of shaping the future of our children, I applaud and congratulate you.

CHAPTER SIX

For Our Children's Sake: Gentle Reminders of Parental Responsibility

Leong Wai Kum

About the Speaker

Professor Leong Wai Kum graduated at the top of her class in the then newly established Faculty of Law, University of Malaya in Kuala Lumpur, Malaysia. She was the Lord President's Scholar. She then proceeded to Harvard University in the US for her graduate studies, before becoming the first graduate of the Faculty of Law, University of Malaya, to join the Faculty of Law, University of Singapore, as lecturer. Today, she is a full Professor in that Faculty, and the University has become the National University of Singapore.

Born in what was then the Federation of Malaya, in Kuala Lumpur, her family is Cantonese, and she recalls that when starting school she did not speak a word of English. Indeed, her family story is that of a hard-working immigrant family of humble origins.

She writes, "My paternal grandfather had sailed from his Sam Sui Village in Canton Province, southern China to Singapore and then crossed over to Selangor, Malaya as a penniless boy. By the time my father married, my grandfather had begun to amass a small fortune by sheer enterprise and hard work. My father demonstrated similar business acumen and entrepreneurship. He had promised his mother on her deathbed that he would cease school at Form Four at the Methodist Boys' School in Kuala Lumpur to help out my grandfather in his burgeoning tailoring business. That put an end to my father's formal education. He possessed enough drive to do a correspondence course with a Tailoring Institute in London, UK, leading to his certification as a master cutter. To today's brand-aware consumers, my father could style himself a bespoke tailor. This was no mean achievement by a young man living in Malaya in the 1940s. The tailoring business prospered under my father's charge as there were many British army officers to suit up in Kuala Lumpur."

Professor Leong now dedicates herself to teaching and writing. She takes every opportunity to contribute to improving the family law in Singapore, having participated in the major revisions of the Women's Charter, our main family law statute, in 1979 and 1995. She has written a great deal on this subject, collectively published in the form of the first law CD-ROM by a single author, entitled *The Family Law Library of Singapore*. But most interestingly, she clad the second edition of her *Elements of Family Law in Singapore*, published in 2012, in a jacket that reproduced the marriage certificate of the traditional marriage of her parents in 1940 (which we reproduce in the text). The book contains a loving explanation of the details of this cover, and the history of the couple, from which the excerpt quoted above is taken. Lawyers do not, as a class, stand out for their originality and departure from convention, but a more creative way to enclose a book on family law would be hard to imagine.

Leong Wai Kum's other interest is the impact of law on women in Singapore. In this connection she co-managed a major local interdisciplinary research project, to establish the baselines that culminated in the publication *Singapore Women: Three Decades of Change*, in 1993. This work was co-edited with Aline Wong, who is the speaker in the 4th Singapore Children's Society Lecture (Chapter 4).

Professor Leong has a distinguished reputation but she is no ivory-tower academic. In 2011, to commemorate the 50th year of operation of the Women's Charter, Professor Leong wrote *The Women's Charter:*

50 Questions, published by the Institute of Southeast Asian Studies, Singapore. This practical book asks and answers 50 questions that a member of the general public might have of this statute, which regulates several important parts of our lives. It was launched by the Association of Women for Action and Research (AWARE) in March 2011, the year before the present lecture was delivered. Speaking at the launch she remarked that, "The Women's Charter is by no means perfect but it is pretty darn good, in my opinion." She called Section 46 of the Charter (which states that by marrying, both husband and wife are in an equal and cooperative partnership bringing each other's different efforts together for mutual benefit) a remarkable provision as it paints the ideal picture of what a marriage should be but does not enforce any punishment on the couple should any party fail to live up to the ideal. Professor Leong took the opportunity of the Singapore Children's Society Lecture to elaborate this view, but extending it to consider what the legal regulation of parenting means for children.

Leong Wai Kum as a P4 schoolgirl

The 6th Lecture, delivered 29 September 2012

I shall try to make three points in this lecture:[1]

— How the law in Singapore regulates parents and parenting,
— Give a report card on the state of the law, and
— Suggest one improvement.

The Law in Singapore Regulating Parents and Parenting

The basic principles of the law regulating parents and parenting are found in the Women's Charter that is the core family statute in Singapore.[2] The law does not regulate parenting directly, for example by arranging for someone to monitor each parent–child

One of the most unusual book covers ever published? The Speaker's parents' Wedding Certificate enhancing the cover of her book on family law. Image courtesy of LexisNexis.

---

[1] A fully referenced academic paper based on this lecture may be found as Leong Wai Kum, "Prohibiting Parental Physical Discipline of Child in Singapore", *Singapore Academy of Law Journal* 26, no. 2 (2014), 499–519. In this chapter, the references have been reduced for ease of reading by the lay reader.

[2] The Women's Charter is now Chapter 353 of the 2009 Revised Edition of the Statutes of the Republic of Singapore. It was enacted as the State of Singapore Ordinance 18 of 1961 where the current section 46(1) was section 45(1).

relationship every minute of the day. This is simply unworkable and, even if workable, could do greater harm than good. The law, instead, regulates it more subtly. It cajoles parents to discharge their parenting in a moral manner to the best of the parents' ability and always for the benefit of the child.

Since the enactment of the Women's Charter in 1961, section 46(1) proclaims:

> Upon the solemnization of marriage, the husband and the wife shall be mutually bound to co-operate with each other in safe-guarding the interests of the union and in caring and providing for the children.

Our core family statute thus reminds married people that there are two relationships they should nurture within their marriage. It is not only their own marital relationship that the spouses should build up but also their relationship with their child (as individual parents and as a couple) that should be treasured and nurtured. The law directs the spouses that, as parents, they are both bound to co-operate with each other to care for their children. Their parenthood is expressed as their joint responsibility towards their children.

The significance of parental responsibility is better appreciated when we remember that, prior to the enactment of section 46(1), the common law that used to apply here conveyed parenthood as a series of rights the parents owned over their children. In Singapore, then, parental rights have been superseded by parental respon-sibility for the last 50 years.

Compared with parental rights, parental responsibility conveys parenthood very differently. Parenthood is now conveyed morally as responsibility. A moral tone is appropriate in legal regulation of parents. The way we behave has as much to do with what the law demands of us as how the law expresses these demands. There is a lot of benefit from the law saying to parents that its view of the parent–child relationship is of the parents owing responsibility to the child. While parents naturally possess and exercise authority over their children (and this follows simply from the way society is organised around nuclear families), the parental authority is expressed by the law as responsibility. A parent owes responsibility towards his or her child and he or she exercises authority in order to discharge this responsibility.

It is not every family statute in every country that contains such a clear statement of what parenting is. This is a noteworthy feature of the law in Singapore. We should give credit to the drafters of the original Women's Charter, who had enough foresight to appreciate the value of introducing such change in the law regulating parenting as early as 50 years ago.

The idea of parenthood being based upon parental responsibility only gained international recognition when the United Nations sponsored its Convention on the Rights of the Child (UNCRC) in 1989. The UNCRC has the distinction of being the most widely ratified international document, to which only the US, Somalia and South Sudan still fail to commit. Singapore ratified it on 4 November 1995 albeit with some reservations. By its Article 3(2), "States Parties undertake to ensure the child such protection and care as is necessary for his or her wellbeing, taking into account the rights and duties of his or her parents." This Article is widely acknowledged to require States Parties to commit to entrenching parental responsibility in their laws.

Since the UNCRC, many countries have come to adopt this moral way of regulating parenthood. Many countries in Europe have changed their laws to this modern basis. In England, for example, the (UK) Children Act 1989 also adopted the idea of parental responsibility in place of the old idea of parental rights. The law in Singapore may be thought to have a head start over the laws in many countries by a few decades.

There is a huge difference across different cultures in terms of how parenting happens — the way that western culture does it, the way that Asian culture does it. What is your opinion of "tiger mom" parenting?

I would respond by saying that actually I disagree with you. We talk a lot about our cultural differences but I think that at the end of the day we are far more similar than we are different. Certainly as far as parental discipline of children is concerned, it has been shown to be a global phenomenon. If I hadn't looked into it, I would have thought it is an Asian phenomenon that we should be disciplined, our children should be disciplined, toughened up; and part and parcel of it is such parenting. But I think that every society, across all cultures, would say that the tiger mom, well, that's extreme. And to that extent, I repeat that I think we are actually far more similar, as people, than we are different.

— From the Question & Answer session

Parental responsibility in section 46(1) of the Women's Charter is supported by another statutory provision that requires any decision or official action taken towards a child to be guided by what is in the "welfare of the child". In this way the provision in section 46(1) gains practical enforceability.

The Guardianship of Infants Act[3] section 3 requires any court to decide every question relating to the "upbringing of an infant" by considering what is in the "welfare of the infant as the first and paramount consideration". This is a pointedly singular direction and it applies extremely broadly. Its effect on a parent is that, if any action by a parent becomes subject to court scrutiny, it must

---

[3] Originally enacted as the Straits Settlements Guardianship of Infants Ordinance 11 of 1934; the current version is Cap 122, 1985 Rev Ed.

be found to be in pursuit of the welfare of the child. The direction applies equally to an action by a non-parent and subjects it to a similar requirement. Any action that is found to fall short of pursuing the welfare of the child risks not receiving the court's endorsement. Where appropriate, the court can order that a flawed or unlawful action be undone and substituted by action that achieves the welfare of the child.

The opening words of section 46(1) may be thought to limit it to married parents. The Court of Appeal in *Lim Chin Huat Francis v Lim Kok Chye Ivan*,[4] however, may have extended parental responsibility beyond married parents. The case concerned two sets of adults, who were not the biological parents of the young girl involved, seeking the court's order to obtain the physical possession of her. The Court of Appeal decided not to change the child's *status quo*. In the course of his judgment, the then Chief Justice Yong Pung How observed that the court would demand demonstration of responsibility from these adults who were merely hoping to be appointed her adoptive parents. In other words, section 46(1) of the Women's Charter can be read to extend the expectation of parental responsibility, to the extent it is appropriate, to people hoping to become parents. This bold reading would surely mean that all parents and not just married parents, i.e., unmarried, separated and divorced parents are included within section 46(1).

Parents by law bear the responsibility to co-operate in caring and providing for their children. From the 1960s, the law in Singapore expects married, unmarried, separated, or divorced parents (a) to view their child as someone towards whom they owe responsibility; (b) to discharge the responsibility co-operatively with the other parent and/or guardian; and (c) to do so for the purpose of achieving the welfare of the child. By an extended reading, there may be similar expectations for people hoping to become the child's adoptive parents or people voluntarily becoming guardians of a child.

---

[4] [1999] 2 *Singapore Law Reports (R)* 392, particularly at [91].

Family law regulates two relationships that are unique, i.e., that between the spouses and that between parents and their child. Both are emotion-laden. Both last for a long time. The parent–child relationship lasts for their lives while the hope is that the marital relationship will also last for the spouses' lives. Both are comparatively more complex than other relationships. Of the parent–child relationship, it begins in complete dependence of the child upon his or her parents but is dynamic as the child grows and matures each day. These unique qualities of the parent–child relationship require that the law regulating it be sensitive. It is not appropriate to heavy-handedly impose a fixed set of legal obligations as parenting obligations.

The law directs all parents that they should exercise their authority over their child in a co-operative manner. The parents must jointly parent their child. Whether the father or mother is sole breadwinner or sole homemaker and child-carer, or a combination of both, they should co-operate to the best of their ability. In several areas of life, the law even requires that the parents must co-operate, as failure to co-operate is against the law.[5] Co-operative parenting is best for the child as he or she gets the benefit of both parents' input and care.

FOR WHOM THE SCALES FALL?

---

[5] See e.g., *L v L* [1996] 2 *Singapore Law Reports (R)* 529.

The law requires that parenting should be for the wellbeing of the child. It is not for the parents' enjoyment or for them to show "who is boss". If a court is made aware that any exercise of authority by a parent was for a purpose other than in pursuit of the wellbeing of the child, the court can chastise the parent concerned and, in a fit case, can order that the unlawful exercise of parental authority be reversed. There are reported cases where the court has ordered the parent who acted unlawfully to reverse the action.[6] Beyond individual decisions, the law has a salutary effect. It demands that every decision made of a child and every action taken with regard to the child must meet this threshold of being done for the wellbeing of the child. While it is not possible, practically speaking, to be looking over the shoulder and judging every parent every minute of the day, it is nevertheless useful for the law to make this demand. The more gross failures in parenting can be picked up and the courts have opportunity to propound on what the law demands of all parents.

There is truth to the oft-mentioned statement that "it takes a village to raise a child". The law in Singapore allows all of us to bring any gross failure of parenting that we are aware of to the attention of the court, directly, or to the Ministry of Social and Family Development where the Protector of children is entrusted with the public care of children. The operating principle is that court proceedings can be swiftly and easily convened. Once convened, however, the judge will make the most careful assessment of the situation and make the decision that appears to be the wisest and most helpful to the child. There will be no injudicious intervention in a family that is functioning harmoniously.

The principle that parenting should be jointly discharged is best appreciated within the law of custody and guardianship. When parents separate or divorce it has become common for each parent to seek not only court orders of the care and control of their

---

[6] In *L v L* [1996] 2 *Singapore Law Reports (R)* 529, the mother who unlawfully changed her young daughter's surname without first obtaining the agreement of her father was ordered to undo the change.

child, but of custody as well. The 2005 Court of Appeal decision in *CX v CY*[7] marked the culmination of years of development towards optimal relationship between parenthood and guardianship. The Court of Appeal expounded on the need for guardianship to support parental responsibility and never undermine it. To support parental responsibility, two sub-principles of guardianship are needed.

One, it may not always be necessary for the court to order custody of the child even where one or both parents seek such an order. A decision by the court of "no custody order" may be the best outcome of an application made between the parents where there is no pressing disagreement between the parents on how to bring up their child. That the parents have differences of view so that disputes may arise in future is generally not a good enough reason for a custody order. Where no custody order is made, the parents are left to be regulated by section 46(1) of the Women's Charter. Parents making big decisions regarding their child must act consistently with parental responsibility. They must try their best to co-operate to achieve the welfare of their child.

Two, where an order of custody must be made, the court should favour an order of joint custody by the parents instead of an order of sole custody by one parent. An order of sole custody is only justified where there is a need to keep one parent completely out of the child's life. This may be so only where there has been such dereliction of responsibility as the parent having abused the child physically or sexually, or having caused grave emotional abuse. Short of gross dereliction of parental responsibility and particularly where there is hope that an irresponsible parent might learn and improve, there is no good reason to make an order of sole custody that formally shuts that parent out of the child's life.

The principle that parental exercise of authority not for the well-being of the child is unlawful may be best appreciated within the

---

[7]   [2005] 3 *Singapore Law Reports (R)* 690.

unfortunate incidents of parental abduction of children across borders. The Hague Convention on the Civil Aspects of International Child Abduction 1980 is a relatively simple scheme of co-operation among nations of the world. The scheme is for countries to offer help to locate and return an abducted child to the country of the child's habitual residence before the abduction, so that the courts there can decide on the simmering dispute between the child's parents. The Minister for Community Development, Youth and Sports announced in Parliament in early 2010 that the government intended to accede to the Hague Convention.

There can be no doubt that a child should be protected from unlawful parental behaviour in removing him or her out of the jurisdiction of the court of habitual residence. A parent who abducts his or her own child away from the country of the child's habitual residence has grossly failed in his or her responsibility. When this, unfortunately, happens, and the authorities are asked by the other parent to assist, such assistance should be rendered immediately.

The Singapore Parliament enacted the International Child Abduction Act in 2011 in order that our international commitments may be discharged. A Central Authority was created to offer assistance to a parent of a child from another country who has been abducted to Singapore. In return, a Singaporean parent whose child has been abducted abroad can similarly avail himself or herself of facilities created in such overseas countries. Two different steps to assist may be discerned.

First, an application can be made to the Central Authority for assistance in locating the abducted child and then facilitating the voluntary return of the child or an amicable resolution of the dispute relating to the removal or retention of the child. Once the abducted child is located, the ideal is for the child to be voluntarily returned by whoever removed the child from the country of habitual residence. To this end the Act encourages an amicable resolution of the problem.

Where voluntary return is not effected, however, an application to the court may be made as step two for an order that the child be returned to the country of habitual residence. The order will almost always be made, and made speedily. It may only be refused in fairly circumscribed circumstances, *viz.* if the person having care of the child was not actually exercising custody rights at the time of the removal of the child or had consented or acquiesced in the removal; or if there is a grave risk that the child's return would expose the child to physical or psychological harm or otherwise place the child in an intolerable situation; or the child objects to being returned and has attained an age and degree of maturity where it is appropriate to take the child's view into consideration. The idea is for the child to almost always be returned to the country of habitual residence where its courts will then engage in deliberations as long as necessary to make orders that pursue the child's welfare. Any other court should aim only to expeditiously return the child to his or her habitual residence.

Report on the State of Law:
Healthy but Always Room to Improve

The state of the law in Singapore regulating parents and their relationship with their children is healthy. It may be in a better state than the equivalent law in other countries. There is, however, always room for improvement. For the sake of our children, it helps to make gentle reminders of parental responsibility every now and then. Every gentle reminder that parenthood is a privilege is timely and useful, so that parental responsibility is discharged as well as the parent is capable of. In this connection I completely support the courses on good parenting that many centres in Singapore offer continuously. Each of us can learn more of how to be the best parent we can be. By the same token as healthy as the state of the law regulating parents and parenting is, there is always room for improvement.

One Improvement: Stop Physical Punishment of the Child as a Means of Discipline

I would like to suggest one change to the law. This change will stop parents in Singapore from inflicting physical punishment on their children for any reason including as a means of discipline of the child. We can all learn to teach our children discipline in ways that do not involve physical punishment.

There is a global initiative to end all corporal punishment of children, including by their parents, that is dedicated to "forge a strong alliance of human rights agencies, key individuals and international and national non-governmental organisations against corporal punishment" and "promote awareness-raising of children's rights to protection and public education on positive, non-violent forms of discipline for children".[8] The initiative has support from, among others, the Committee on the Rights of the Child, which regards several articles of the UNCRC as prohibiting corporal punishment of a child. It is also recommended to the Council of Europe to direct holders of parental responsibility that a child should not be subjected to corporal punishment or any other humiliating treatment. We have to consider the global initiative seriously. I would like to see Singapore legislate an addition to the Women's Charter section 46(1) to discourage all parents from the infliction of corporal punishment of their children.

It is important that we put this initiative in its proper context. Studies have shown that it is a global phenomenon. Most societies habitually allow parents to discipline their children including by inflicting moderate physical punishment.

In Singapore the common law protects the parent who inflicts moderate physical punishment on his or her child in the name of discipline. Such behaviour is condoned as legitimate exercise of parental authority. Further, the Women's Charter that offers protection

---

[8] See *Global Initiative to End All Corporal Punishment of Children* at www.endcorporalpunishment.org, accessed 18 July 2015.

from all conduct of "family violence" exempts "any force lawfully used … by way of correction towards a child below 21 years of age".[9] Beyond moderate physical punishment, of course, the parent runs against the criminal law that protects the child from all physical and, even, emotional and psychological harm.

The global initiative is moved by the view that every society should review this practice and decide whether it is acceptable any longer. We should not think that disciplining a child by physical punishment is, somehow, an Asian tradition. It is not restricted to Asia. All societies have been tolerating parental infliction of moderate physical punishment of their children. It is now time for all societies to look more closely into the practice.

There is incontrovertible evidence from social science studies that physical punishment of a child by any person in authority, including by a parent, does more harm to the child than any perceived good.[10] A summary of the scientific evidence finds "a large and consistent body of research from countries around the world that leads to two clear conclusions":[11]

> First, corporal punishment is no better than other methods of discipline at gaining immediate or long-term child compliance. Second, corporal punishment is not predictive of any intended positive outcomes for children and, in contrast, is significantly predictive of a range of negative, unintended consequences, with the demonstrated risk for physical injury being the most concerning. On balance, the risk of harm far outweighs any short-term good.

The child learns the wrong lesson from a parent using violence on him or her. A bigger and more powerful person using violence on a child is not right under any circumstances.

---

[9] See section 64 in its definition of what conduct constitutes the commission of family violence.
[10] See, e.g., Elizabeth T. Gershoff, "More Harm than Good: A Summary of Scientific Research on the Intended and Unintended Effects of Corporal Punishment on Children", Law and Contemporary Problems 73, no. 31 (2010), 31–56.
[11] Ibid., 55.

The Committee on the Convention of the Rights of the Child regards the continued corporal punishment of children as against the Convention. The Committee points to several Articles of the Convention that require States that have committed to the UNCRC to take steps to prohibit corporal punishment of a child.

Article 37(a) lays down the right of the child not to be subjected to cruel, inhuman, or degrading treatment or punishment. This may be regarded as supplemented by Article 16 that lays down the right of the child not to be subjected to unlawful attacks on his or her honour and reputation as well as the right to protection from such attacks. Such provisions protect both the dignity and the physical and mental integrity of the child. Article 40(1) specifically refers to the dignity of the child. States parties are required to ensure that a child, including one accused of committing a crime, be treated so as to promote the child's sense of dignity and worth in order to reinforce the child's respect for basic human rights and the fundamental freedoms of others. As Singapore has committed to the UNCRC since 1995, she should give the utmost consideration to the view of the Committee that the UNCRC does prohibit corporal punishment of a child.

Many forward-looking countries have accordingly changed their laws, although it should also be said that many others are still dragging their feet. Among those that have made changes, these can come in different forms.

Sweden is always cited as the first country in the world to act, indeed even before the UNCRC. In 1979 Sweden enacted law to prohibit corporal punishment of children by anyone including by their parents by adding this to their Parenthood and Guardianship Code: "A child may not be subjected to corporal punishment or other injurious or humiliating treatment." This continues to be held out as the gold standard and much has been written about this enlightened legislation. It is often pointed out that Sweden too had traditionally regarded it as part of the privilege of parenting to use moderate physical punishment in discipline. What interests me the most is the comment that the legislation (including discussion of whether to enact the law) had tremendous effect on changing societal perception. In 1965 the percentage of adult Swedes who considered physical punishment of a child as occasionally necessary was 53%; this began falling to 42% in 1968 and further to 39% in 1971. After the law was enacted and the Swedish government took steps to increase public knowledge of the ban, by 1981, only 26% still regarded corporal punishment as an acceptable part of parenting.[12] Closer to home, Thailand has taken several steps to limit corporal punishment of children[13] in schools, as a sentencing option in courts, and as a disciplinary step in institutions, although it stopped short of banning its use at home.

Is physical punishment worse than other forms of distressing punishment that are psychological in their character rather than physical?

I think most people would agree that physical punishment of children should first and foremost be prohibited, whether or not we later proceed to prohibit other things. My view is simply that physical punishment is more visible, and that is the way of distinguishing one form of abuse from another. If we enter into discussions about whether a child has been emotionally abused and so on, that kind of discussion is far more sophisticated than a discussion of physical punishment. It is not that I think physical punishment is worse than the other forms, I think it is just easier for the law to manage, to control, the more visible forms of punishment of children.

— *From the Question & Answer session*

---

[12] See, e.g., Dennis Alan Olson, "The Swedish Ban of Corporal Punishment", *Brigham Young University Law Review*, 1984, no. 3 (1984), 447–456.

[13] See Leslee Nelson, Maggie Honrath, Laura Lacci, and Kelley Menzano, "Corporal Punishment of Children in Thailand: An International Illustration on the Challenges of Confronting the Final Frontier" *Children's Legal Rights Journal* 29, no. 2 (2009), 9–33.

We in Singapore should begin from the recognition that the law is in a good state compared with that in many countries. From this healthy perch, what I suggest we do is to enact law to make this small change to parenting. Given that the law already sets parenting within a moral framework and directs parents to exercise their authority over their children in order to pursue the well-being of their children, the next logical step is to enact law to stop the physical punishment of children at home. We can start on this as painlessly (pun intended) as possible. There is no need yet to punish a breach of this new law. The new law should be widely disseminated. Equally important, its enactment should be accompanied by information and teaching by child psychologists of the better alternative means of disciplining the child. Parents should be given the time to learn the new paradigm. It is not right to use any amount of force upon a child. Where it is not lawful for a person to inflict any amount of force upon the body of an adult, how can the infliction of the same amount of force on the body of a child be acceptable? When the message has become widely known, then only should we think of what may be the appropriate next step forward.

If we do not believe in physical punishment, can we use verbal abuse?

I would say that once we have taken care of physical punishment, we have moved up a notch and then we can consider what else might not be acceptable. So in theory, verbal abuse is something to be considered, although as a lawyer I'm always very cognizant that there is such a thing as going too far. Parenting is something that must be done by the parents on the spot, and the law cannot keep heaping requirements upon parents to the point where it makes parenting too difficult a process.

— From the Question & Answer session

Conclusion

In my opinion it is completely consistent with the state of the law in Singapore regulating parents for the law to prohibit a parent's use of physical force upon his or her child. We can begin by prohibiting the conduct without necessarily subjecting the erring parent to any punishment himself or herself. We can rightly follow the spirit of the Women's Charter section 46(1) to put in place a legal requirement of parents that desists from punishing an erring parent. Family law, which regulates the delicate relationship between the parents and child, is often improved by the judicious use of a carefully crafted legal expectation that may not punish failure of compliance. Such a law will subtly but no less surely influence parenting in a positive way. The law regulating parents will be improved and we can all take immense pride in the law being expressed in the optimal fashion for the good of all our children.

CHAPTER SEVEN

The Modern Dilemma: Reconciling Children, Family and Career

Halimah Yacob

About the Speaker

The Honourable Mdm Halimah Yacob is the Speaker of Parliament, the ninth to hold that high office, which she assumed in January 2013. A lawyer by profession, she was called to the bar in 1981, having graduated from NUS in the class of 1978, which she attended as a MUIS Scholar. She is also an old girl of Tanjong Katong Girls' School, and, perhaps unexpectedly, the Singapore Chinese Girls' School. A longstanding and active trade unionist, she rose from humble beginnings to become an MP in 2001, followed by Minister of State in the then Ministry of Community Development, Youth and Sports, before her present position. Her early life was not at all easy, with her father, the family breadwinner, passing away when she was eight. Tellingly, in an interview for LawLink (for the NUS Law Faculty alumni) she remarked that, "Maybe because of my own background, my primary attraction to law was because it provided an avenue to seek justice for the downtrodden and defenceless, although we know that in the real world this can sometimes be too idealistic."

For this reason, too, she recognised early on the work of the NTUC as something worth supporting, and went into Union work after graduating, instead of into a private law firm. Her comments on this bear repeating. "NTUC", she said, "was a natural stop for me as what NTUC stood for was consistent with my own values and beliefs. Workers need a voice to balance against the stronger bargaining position of employers. Sometimes people do not appreciate the role of NTUC and its unions. The unionists really work very hard to represent the workers' interest in a very competitive global situation." These are the words of the former NTUC Deputy Secretary-General, Director of the Legal Services Department, and Director of the Women's Development Secretariat. She has also served as the Executive Secretary of the United Workers of Electronics and Electrical Industries and on various boards including the Housing and Development Board, Tripartite Alliance on Fair Employment Practices, Tripartite Workgroup on Enhancing Employment Choices for Women, and MENDAKI Sense.

Halimah Yacob has several "firsts" to her name. She is the first Malay woman to be elected an MP, the first female Speaker of Parliament and the longest serving female Muslim MP. She was the first Singaporean to be elected to the governing body of the International Labour Organisation (ILO).

Though married with five children, Mdm Halimah manages to combine work and home life, and is uniquely qualified to speak to her chosen topic of reconciling children, family and a career. Reflecting on the lecture, in late 2014, she reiterated something that she also said in response to a question from the floor — that sometimes people expect too much of a government. Governments can only do so much; they can enable people, but they cannot manage family life.

The Children's Society, she felt, could contribute by encouraging family conversations about practical issues that affected many families, such as the importance of fathers and their changing roles, or how to discipline children in a new and more relaxed modern environment.

Indeed, she wondered if a one-stop centre for advice on parenting and children might be a suitable remit to include in the Society's brief. Similarly, investigating social differences and the limits to social mobility would be a useful endeavour if it led to ways to reduce stratification in society.

Mdm Woo Yun Sum (left) with the Speaker at the Singapore Women's Association lunch, March 2015

Source: *The Straits Times* © Singapore Press Holdings Limited. Reprinted with permission.

The 7th Lecture, delivered 5 October 2013

Reconciling children, family and career in today's context appears to be a gargantuan task. Can we ever reconcile them or do we accept that these are irreconcilable objectives and learn to live with these imperfections? There are no easy answers, yet the wellbeing of our families, and in particular of our children, depends a great deal on how effectively we are able to deal with one of modern society's most challenging conundrums.

To effectively tackle this challenge requires a coordinated and concerted effort at the policy level, as well as at reshaping society's attitudes and mindsets towards the roles of men and women, particularly in caregiving responsibilities. We also need to recognise that there is no "one size fits all" solution, something that we are so fond of seeking, because the problem is complex and multifaceted with different families affected differently, depending also on their household income.

Among all the factors that have led to this dilemma, two significant changes growing in tandem have been taking place in our society, one in the family and the other in the workplace. We need to understand these changes to develop effective strategies to help people cope better.

Changes in the Family

In the family, a quiet revolution has been taking place. In the first half of the last century, roles within the family between men and women were clearly defined. These gendered roles, imposed through years of socialisation, were those where the woman was the caregiver and the man was the wage earner. Many of the mothers in my generation never worked, unless they were forced to because of the death of the breadwinner; as in my case, for my mother had to work when my father died, and I was eight years old. In such cases, work was not a matter of choice but something that had to be done out of necessity.

By the middle of the century, the roles had begun to change, particularly among the women. Women had access to education and began to enter the workforce and assume the wage earner's role as well. In Singapore, the labour force participation rate of women in the prime working ages of 25 to 54 years increased from 65.2% in 2002 to 75.7% in 2011. This is a high figure, quite comparable to that in other developed countries. Although more women were entering the workforce, the rules, which were developed with men as the sole breadwinner in mind, remained unchanged. For example, like men, women are also working longer, which is why there is also a greater demand for childcare, because grandmothers, who had traditionally provided childcare support to working mothers, are no longer able to do so.

Also, even as women began to take on more paid work outside the home, their role beyond paid work remained unchanged. They continued to do most of the housework and continued to be the main caregiver for their children. There are no detailed studies on this, but it appears that on average, parents in Singapore spend about 29 hours with their children every week. Mothers, however, spend significantly more time with their children, about 34 hours per week compared to fathers who do 24 hours per week. These hours refer only to time spent with the children. They don't tell us how much time women spent on housework, although there are International Labour Organisation (ILO) studies which indicate that globally, working women spend a lot more time on housework compared to men. In another local survey, out of 19 domestic chores covering childcare, homecare and supervision, and eldercare, women reported carrying out an average of 8.8 of these 19 tasks compared to an average of 2.7 for men. Men took the lead only in three tasks, namely household repairs, washing the car and paying the bills. As someone said, "This is the cultural contradiction of modern motherhood. Mothers assume the co-provider role but still feel compelled to be 'all giving' and 'ever available' to their children. Being a good mother devoted to one's children is a core identity that does not change when women take on more hours of paid work."

When I became a Member of Parliament in 2001, I was often asked, and mind you most of the time by women themselves, who was going to take care of my children. My response to them was, "Why don't you ask the male MPs that question?" That helped, because after a while, people stopped asking me that question. The expectations and stereotypes of male and female roles are so ingrained that no one even cared to think about parenting as a shared responsibility despite all the progress that we have made.

To be fair to Singaporean fathers, in a Fatherhood Perception Survey conducted in 2009,[1] many indicated that they knew they were spending less time with their children but wanted to do more. However, 63% said that they were hampered from doing so because of their work responsibilities and 53% could not do so because of financial difficulties or pressures.

Yet another change that is taking place in our families and causing this modern day dilemma is our rapidly ageing population,

---

[1] *Singapore Fatherhood Public Perception Survey 2009.* Singapore: Ministry of Community Development, Youth and Sports.

which has increased demand for the care of parents and older relatives. According to the Ministry of Health's National Health Survey 2010,[2] 8.1% of Singapore residents aged between 18 and 69, or about 210,000 people, were providing regular care to sick or frail family members. On average, they provided 6.8 hours of care per day. A slightly higher proportion of them were women and the majority of the caregivers, 69% of them, were married. About 75% of them were employed. This suggests that most caregivers juggle caregiving tasks with work commitments and family responsibilities, which is a real struggle.

Another factor that affects work–life balance is divorce. Single-parent households struggle because they have less income and usually only one adult to take care of the children. In this instance, the single parent, usually the mother, becomes both the earner and caregiver for the family, and her struggle to balance work and family is even more daunting. In the United States, about 25% of households is headed by single parents. The number of single-parent households is climbing in Singapore although perhaps not yet as high as the US. There are no published figures in Singapore on single-parent households, although the number of divorces and annulments is rising, from 5,071 in 2001 to 7,604 in 2011.

The NTUC Women's Development Secretariat has published a guide[3] for single mothers, and their research suggests that seven in 10 of the single mums were not educated beyond upper secondary, eight in 10 of the single mums work, with the majority of them working full-time, and a third of them earn less than $1,000 per month. The single mums indicated that they needed help mainly in financial and employment issues and for their children's development. Many also indicated that their children are affected not only by the lack of financial support but because, as single parents, they also struggle to fulfil their children's emotional needs.

---

[2] *National Health Survey 2010.* Singapore: Epidemiology and Disease Control Division, Ministry of Health.

[3] *Going Solo: A Guide for Single Mothers* (Singapore: NTUC Women's Development Secretariat, 2009 — available in English and Mandarin).

I have just returned to work after my maternity leave and was told I would not be considered for promotion because I went on maternity leave. How would you deal with such a situation?

This is a real issue. Fortunately, when I had my five children, it was when I was with NTUC, the labour movement. There we must practise what we preach so it didn't affect my promotion opportunity. But when we wanted to extend maternity benefit from two months to three months to four months, we had conversations with the women and they gave me two sides of the story. Women who support said, *Yes this is very important because we need to have more time to bond with the baby and to spend time with the family.* But there are other women whose workplace is female-dominated and they said, *Look, we do have a real problem when you extend the maternity leave.* And if you take four months of paid maternity benefits and if you also take childcare leave, against an employee who does not consume that leave, and with performance being equal, you cannot expect a bigger bonus or to be promoted faster than her. We do have to accept some trade-offs. But this is for that year only; you don't give birth every year, right? So a job is a long-term career. If it affects you for the long term then that's being unreasonable and unfair. But for the short term you have to expect that there will be some trade-offs that you have to live with.

— From the Question & Answer session

Changes in the Workplace

Even as changes are taking place in our family that impact on work–life balance, the effect is compounded by the way that work is structured and the limited options that are available to working parents. It is well known that we work very long hours, in fact, one of the longest in the world. In 2012, Singaporeans worked 45.6 hours in a week; but this included part-time work as well. If only full-time work is taken into consideration, we worked 48.2 hours weekly. Such long working hours make work–life balance very challenging. At the same time, the labour market is also a lot more fragmented, contributing to the instability in families. In 2012, no fewer than 192,200 or 11.5% of workers were on term contracts. Another 196,800 or 9.6% worked as part-timers, although some could have opted to do so voluntarily. The challenge with part-time work is that it pays low wages and provides poor fringe benefits.

There is now greater inequality in the growth of wages. In 2000, the average monthly household income of those at the 11th to the 20th percentile was $2,241. This figure rose to $3,302 in 2012. For those at the 81st to 90th percentile, their average monthly household income was $9,461 in 2000 and it rose to $16,366 in 2012.

Hence, the impact of long hours of work on families differs depending on their income levels, something which we have to bear in mind when we work out the solutions. For the lower-income families, the solution is to ensure that they have the skills and are able to earn enough to feed their family. They also need more holistic support for their children, especially in caregiving, when long hours of work keep them away from home and there is no one to supervise the children. Studies have shown that in low-income families, when both parents have to work, it is the older siblings that end up having to take care of the younger ones, sometimes at the expense of their own education. For middle- or upper-income families, with more disposable incomes to purchase the services that can reduce their burden in caregiving, their big challenge is the lack of flexibility at the workplace. They may need time to cater to their children's developmental needs, such as sending them to enrichment programmes, which they may not have the time to do.

There is a law passed in Germany recently that restricts the employer from calling the employee after office hours. Can Singapore do the same, to send a strong signal to the employers?

How many of you supervise staff? Do you send emails after working hours? You do, right? You are the culprits! No need to wait for a law. You can do something now.

I am also a culprit. I sometimes send emails late at night, but I do tell my people, *I don't expect responses at the same time that I send. You can reply tomorrow morning.* So start from yourself and also limit yourself on social media. Facebook and other media eat a lot into your family time. I went to eat with my daughter the other day and it was a buffet lunch. There was this mother and her son. I think a 10-year-old boy. They were not talking to each other. They were talking to their handphones. When you go to restaurants and hawker centres, look around you and see what other people are doing. They are always pressing something. Always pressing something, and then they worry why their children are not talking to them and not listening to them. Such children can't talk to people outside the family either. So we need to check ourselves also. My children impose a ruling on me. *If we go on holiday, please put your iPad in the hotel; don't you ever dare bring your iPad along. If you do bring your iPad along, we'll refuse to go with you out of the hotel.* That helps because otherwise you'll start checking on your work all the time and it is not very helpful.

16 cafes are promoting family bonding by charging 10 per cent less if you dine at their premises with your parents or grandparents

To get the discount, post a photo of yourself and your family at the cafe on Instagram:

After that, everyone can go back to doing what they usually do during meals:

Source: The Straits Times © Singapore Press Holdings Limited. Reprinted with permission.

— From the Question & Answer session

What Has Been Done?

Much has been done, particularly over the last few years, to support families in their dual functions of earning and care-giving, although a lot of the measures are usually delivered in the context of efforts to promote procreation. With the enhancements to the Marriage and Parenthood Package in January 2013, working parents with children aged seven to 12 years were given two days of paid extended childcare leave. Fathers were given one week of paid paternity leave and there was one week of shared parental leave where

---

What is your take on inculcating family values in kids, so that they themselves can help within the family, such as by being more responsible and taking over household tasks, which will help the mothers?

I think that is a truly excellent point. I was at a forum for secondary school kids and the panel members asked, *how many of you made your bed this morning? Put up your hands.* There were about 300 of them and only five lifted their hands. You are really, really right; we need to inculcate those values. Parents always think, *my children must study; it's very important. They've got their exams and assessments and so on.* But over time we completely relieve them from any form of responsibilities at home, making their own beds, helping in the housework, taking care of grandpa, grandma.

The answer lies with the parents, with us. Somehow I think we disempower ourselves. Then when the children say *school work!* We say, *okay you go and study and don't do work.* No. We have to make them assume some responsibilities because they are part of the family and they must feel part of the family. If they don't assume responsibilities now, how are they going to assume responsibilities later towards the family?

— From the Question & Answer session

---

fathers could share one week of the working mother's maternity leave entitlement. Adoptive parents could also get four weeks of paid adoption leave.

The government has also announced that 200 more child care centres will be built in high demand areas over the next few years. Currently, there are 1,051 centres with 97,285 children. Of particular significance to low-income families, more before- and after-school care services will also be provided, to ensure that the children are properly supervised when parents are at work. The pre-school sector is also undergoing tremendous changes with the establishment of the Early Childhood Development Agency (ECDA), and its focus on providing good quality pre-school services will be of greater benefit to the low-income families. I also like the announcement in the 2013 budget, that more funds and resources will be injected into the Learning Support Programme in schools to support weaker students in English and Mathematics.

The Ministry of Manpower has also recently rolled out the Work-Pro Scheme aimed at helping employees benefit from good work–life practices. When I was in the NTUC, we launched a programme called Back2Work with U, and this assisted thousands of women to return to work. So there are measures in place to partially address the changes in the family and at the workplace which have contributed to this modern-day dilemma.

What More Can We Do?

However, more can be done to address these changes, specifically in three areas.

First, we need stronger and more encompassing public messaging to support families in dealing with their dual responsibilities. Currently, the various schemes announced have all been placed under the Marriage and Parenthood Package. Whilst there is nothing wrong in doing this, and a more focussed approach would also help to highlight the problems that we face with our declining birth rate, the flip side is that the message is not inclusive, as it does not include those for whom the procreation target is not applicable. One example would be singles who are the main wage earners and caregivers of their frail parents or disabled siblings, who feel excluded from the messages of flexibility at work and support for the family. A more encompassing message that stresses support for all workers with family obligations would cover a lot more situations that are currently excluded.

You mention that parents should take full responsibility for children's development and not pass the buck to the schools, but there seem to be many parents who send their children to many enrichment activities with no space for free play.

You are really right. I think as parents we have to be discerning. Parents seem to think there is some magic formula that entails sending children to ballet, piano, clarinet, everything. The best thing actually is spending time with your children, and not *making other people spend time with your children*. You know, when you send them here, there, and everywhere you get so harassed that you don't have time to talk to them, to ask them what they want and have deeper conversations with them. You don't have the time. So the answer lies with you. I don't have all the answers, because each of us must be able to see what are our children's needs and how best to develop them.

— From the Question & Answer session

Second, we need to strengthen support for families at the workplace. The government's move in legislating paid childcare leave and paternity leave, as well as longer maternity leave, was a clear recognition that leaving it to the market alone to decide such benefits is not sufficient. Clear legislation was needed to shape and influence behaviour at the workplace to support families. For the same reason, it would be really helpful for families if family-care leave or eldercare leave is also legislated, as caregiving of the frail elderly has increasingly become a big strain on work–life balance. The beauty of legislation for maternity/paternity and childcare leave is that it gives a very strong signal to employers that the government supports employees with childcare obligations. Legislating family-care or eldercare leave will send a similarly strong signal to employers of the government's support for employees with other types of caregiving responsibilities. Such a strong signalling will create more options for those with family obligations, beyond childcare, that take care of their needs instead of options which focus only on the needs of the company.

Besides family and eldercare leave, how about legislating flexible work arrangements?

If we can legislate it that would be the ideal, but I don't think that will be the solution at the present moment. We need to make flexi-work even more effective. We need to identify the issues and challenges. Small and medium-size companies in particular don't have the manpower or specialised human resource departments to work out strategies for them.

Sometimes we may feel that we are actually discriminating against ourselves. The best thing is to raise the issue with your supervisors, your managers and assure them that whatever flexible work arrangements you have will not affect your work output or outcome; that's the most important thing. Many workplaces today are still just measuring face time. You come to work, I look at you, I think you are working, but whether you are surfing the net or what, nobody knows. The way work is assessed is really important. How do we assess work such that we look at the outcome instead of just the face time?

— *From the Question & Answer session*

While we have available support at our workplace, what do you think about the support needed to promote family bonding? While flexible hours help with work–life balance among families with children, what if the cost of living is too high and the wages of flexi-work do not meet the demand of living costs?

One of the challenges we face with part-time work, and also to some extent flexi-work, is that it doesn't pay well. This is a real structural issue which has an impact on families, because if parents are doing work which is not paying well, they will obviously end up having to work for very long hours. These long hours affect their ability to spend time with their children. So we need to make sure that the options that are available actually do pay people well and do provide that kind of fringe benefits, flexible benefits, that can support the family.

Family bonding is a big challenge, I agree, especially when both parents are working. But I have seen many families that are able to do it. Sometimes they also bring in their extended family members, which is where we are also lacking because we don't invest enough time in developing relationships. It is very important to invest in relationships with your family members, with grandparents, with uncles, aunties.

— From the Question & Answer session

Strengthening the workplace also includes making it easier for people to make use of flexi-work options. As a *New York Times* article[4] reported, there continues to be an unspoken stigma about workplace flexibility. It quoted Ms Joan C. Williams, founding director of the Centre for WorkLife Law at the University of California: "Many times these policies are on the books, but informally everyone knows you are penalised for using them."

---

[4] Tara S. Bernard, "The Unspoken Stigma of Workplace Flexibility", *The New York Times*, 15 June 2013, page B1.

Perhaps this explains why flexibility, which includes telecommuting, compressed work weeks and sharing jobs among employees, for example, is still not so popular in Singapore; except maybe for the public sector, as I have met many female civil servants with young children who told me that they found this flexi-scheme useful.

Yet another aspect of strengthening the workplace is to ensure that we create not just jobs but decent work, a terminology long used in the ILO but which only over the last few years has perhaps become more significant in Singapore. In other words, we have to recognise that one major stress factor for low-income families is that they are not earning enough to support their families and provide adequately for their children. All efforts to upgrade, upskill, and provide access to decent jobs for them would address their concerns about maintaining a balance between work and family.

Third, at the societal level, and this is where Voluntary Welfare Organisations can play an important role, we need to promote shared parenting more strongly. The Singapore Fatherhood Perception Survey 2009[5] showed that public perceptions about fathers are generally positive. In that survey 90% agreed that both parents should share responsibilities of raising children and 97% agreed that fathers have an important role in parenting. However, perceptions about fathers' actual involvement in children's lives differed slightly — 84% agreed that fathers are involved in their children's lives, whilst 77% thought fathers are equally as good at caring for children as mothers. Similarly, despite changing social norms, mothers are perceived to be warmer, more involved in family life, more affectionate, and providing more support and guidance in everyday adolescent life than fathers. Although research has shown that attitudes about gender roles have become more egalitarian over the last few decades, these changes in gender attitudes have not been accompanied by corresponding changes in the allocation of housework and caregiving responsibilities.

---

[5] *Singapore Fatherhood Public Perception Survey 2009*, already cited.

You mention increasing the role of NGOs. Would you like to expand a little bit on your thoughts?

What Singapore Children's Society is doing is really important. There are different kinds of children with different kinds of needs. Children from the upper-income households are probably already in some structured programmes, before and after school. For families who don't have that kind of luxury, Children's Society is very important, as it offers programmes that provide enrichment or support, for children who are coming from dysfunctional families. But the important thing is the engagement of the parents. One thing I find about a lot of NGO programmes, in general, is that engagement of the parents is rather weak. Parents must not think that after they have sent their kids to school, that's it. Or that if they send their children to a Children Society's programme, their job is over. We must make sure that parents remain engaged and feel the responsibility for their children.

— From the Question & Answer session

Conclusion

Everyone, at some point in our life, experiences situations where the demands of family caregiving grow so intense that work and family become a struggle. A whole slew of obligations — whether it is a child who needs care, a spouse who is ill, an older parent who needs support — all link us to our families. But as workers, we are also obligated to our employers, on whom we depend for our income and the other satisfactions that paid work provides. The responsibilities that workers have to their families and to their jobs are both important, and are often in conflict.

However, I want to emphasise that work and family conflict has no one solution because it is not one problem. Some people need better paying jobs to earn more income. Some need to take time off when a child is born without derailing their career.

Others need short-term support to attend to a family crisis. Our challenge is for policymakers working with the community to meet this multiplicity of needs.

In conclusion, I wish to thank the Singapore Children's Society for giving me this opportunity to speak. I applaud you for the wonderful work that you have been doing in meeting the needs of the most vulnerable members of our society, that is, our children. Our children deserve no less than to grow up in strong, stable and balanced families where parents are able to dedicate their best to them.

Surely the pressures facing parents will persist as long as there is a huge differential in income and in social respect between the better paid and the least paid members of society?

I agree that there is too much stratification in our labour market. People don't do certain jobs. They look at these jobs and they say, *these are jobs someone else should be doing*; they don't attract the kind of status, image, the kind of salary, the kind of benefits that will make these jobs a lot more attractive. Yes, our job market is very stratified and we don't have much respect for blue-collar work, which is unfortunate.

In 1968 we introduced the Employment Act, and it replaced three labour ordinances passed by the British. These ordinances segregated white-collar and blue-collar workers. White-collar workers got more annual leave; they got better benefits, better sick leave and so on. So in 1968, the government said, *look, we cannot have this segregation*, and the Employment Act was passed to equalise everybody. But in my view, the real challenge to ensuring greater respect for blue-collar work is basically to enhance the content of the work, the value of the work. This is where job re-design is important, so that the content of the work has higher value added, it pays better, and it attracts more fringe benefits. When these things happen, people will see these distinctions less and less as a matter of these jobs attracting less status and other jobs attracting more status.

It is also very true that parents pressurise their children because they have certain ideas about what kind of jobs they want their children to do. It causes real conflict if parents want them to become doctors, or whatever, but they are not interested. Later on in life, sometimes when they are free from their parents they will pursue their own careers. I have seen such people do very well. But again I say, the solution lies not with the government; it lies with us as parents. We need to be realistic about what our children are able to do or not able to do. It does not mean the more you pressurise them, the better they will become.

I remember when my own child was in kindergarten. I saw this mother dragging her child and scolding the child all the way from the kindergarten to a block of flats. Why? Because the child failed her spelling. This was a five-year-old child, she was absolutely miserable, so can you imagine what she would think about going to school, the kinds of fears and horrors she would suffer. I think the real solution lies in us. We need to be more practical. We also need to manage our own expectations.

What role should educators play in shaping and imparting social and moral values, or even the Singapore core values, to the younger generation?

I think that's an important question. As parents we are the primary givers of values. Our children are with us from the day they are born until before they go to school. So we must be the ones to make sure they have the right values even before they enter school. School can help, obviously, and the Ministry of Education has even now made value-based education one of their priority areas, but that alone is not sufficient. If the school instils all the values but when the children go home those values are contradicted by their parents' values, which are different, then I think it's not very useful. So parents, in my view, have the primary responsibility, and as parents, we must never run away from that responsibility. I believe that the school's job is to reinforce values which are important and when the children come home the values are again reinforced. There is a reinforcing loop all around with regard to values for the children. In my view that is important.

The problem is that if both parents are working, the contact and interactive hours that they have with their children are less. Should primary schools incorporate kindergarten or pre-school provision into their education system?

I don't like the idea of "school-ifying" children at a much younger age. I think it's good for the child to grow with a lot more play, with chances to develop and to discover, and not go into a structured school system. Do we believe values are important? We do! So if we do believe values are important, whatever little time we have, we must impart them. I have seen parents whose children are in primary school, and still the domestic helper is tying their shoelaces. Is that a good example of what we should be instilling in our children? No. If I am the mother, it wouldn't take me two seconds to say, *stop, you've got to tie your own shoelaces. The domestic helper is not here to tie your shoelaces.* Children have to learn this idea of independence and respect for people and the kind of work they do. So no matter how little time we have, I don't believe we cannot instil values in children. We are responsible for our children and we look at other institutions — our schools, our society, and so on — to reinforce those values we have built and developed at home.

I teach in early childhood education. Do you think that the Ministry of Education can think about introducing more values and not just concentrating on writing and the other subjects?

I visited the child care centres in Finland and one of the things that they focus on for the children is ethics. I was wondering how do you teach four-, five-, six-year-old children about ethics? But I saw this teacher telling five-year-old children about the story of the lion and the mouse. How the mouse went scampering over a lion when it was sleeping. The lion caught hold of him. Then the mouse said, *please let me go. If you let me go, one day I might save you.* The lion said, *you puny little thing. Want to save me? Never mind, I let you go; I'm in a good mood today.* And then some time later, the mouse found the lion trapped by a hunter. So the mouse went and bit through the ropes to release the lion. The teacher was enacting the story with props. Then she asked the children, *have you ever helped anybody just like how the mouse helped the lion?* And the children began to talk. Some of them talked because they can verbalise. Some of them like to draw so they drew and some of them wrote. And they had a conversation about helping people, about values.

So it is possible. In our system sometimes we may not sufficiently empower our teachers because we have a prescribed syllabus and we expect them to follow it. But one thing about Finland is that they give a lot of flexibility to the teachers to impart the core messages, the core teaching points. So it can be done, you don't have to wait for anything drastic to be done to overhaul the syllabus. In your own interaction with the children every day, you can do it. Just insert those important teachable points.

— *From the Question & Answer session*

CHAPTER EIGHT

Your Children Are Not Your Children

Janadas Devan

About the Speaker

Janadas Devan is the Director of the Institute of Policy Studies. He was educated at the National University of Singapore and Cornell University in the United States.

He taught English in various institutions in Singapore and the US, and later wrote for various publications in the region, before joining *The Straits Times* in 1997. He served as the paper's leader writer for many years, writing editorials on a wide variety of subjects. He also wrote — under his own name — two weekly columns: one on international relations and the other on language. In 2008, he became the editor of the paper's opinion pages, and, in 2010, became the paper's Associate Editor. He also did a weekly radio broadcast, "Call from America", for Radio Singapore International, from 2000 to 2008, on American life and society. He left *The Straits Times* in July 2012, when he was appointed the Government's Chief of Communications at the Ministry of Communications and Information.

Janadas is the eldest son of the late C V Devan Nair, lifelong trade unionist and the third President of Singapore. Janadas has not shied away from the occasional controversy, becoming well known, or notorious, depending on your perspective, for a robust defence, in 2007, of pluralism and the separation of religion and policy. This was in the context of the continued criminalisation of homosexual acts by consenting males.

In a touching tribute to his father at a memorial service in 2006, Janadas revealed something of the diversity and richness that surrounded him as a child. He said, among much else, that his father had been, in many ways, "… an unusual father. … He was baffled by popular culture, and couldn't understand our tastes. I recall on one occasion he took us to see a James Bond movie, thinking it was a children's adventure story. Ten minutes into the movie, he realised his mistake and yanked us out of the theatre. We ended up watching *The Sound of Music* instead. To this day, every time I hear 'Do, Re, Me, Fa, So, La, Ti, Do', I think of James Bond. But what he had to give us was so immensely rich, we never minded in the least that he didn't resemble the fathers our friends had. He would read to us often from literature. He had a near concert-quality singing voice, and would entertain us with classical Hindi and Bengali songs. And then there were the conversations — far-ranging, informative, endlessly fascinating. He was a wonderful teacher. Never instructing, but pointing; never insisting, but suggesting; never enforcing, but showing."

Coming from such a background, it is hardly surprising that Janadas Devan chose to base his lecture title on a famous poem, the message of which contradicts the usual parental assumption of the need and right to direct the lives of their children. The message of the lecture, like the poem, is on building and letting go, not on controlling and steering and hanging on. It is also about looking to the future.

Indeed, reflecting on his lecture a few months after he delivered it, he mentioned many aspects of current shifts in policy that would add up to a considerable shift in public attitudes if they had their expected impact. He regarded the Applied Study in Polytechnics and ITE Review (ASPIRE) commissioned by and accepted by the Ministry of Education as not just a series of programmes, but as a fundamental cultural change for the government, parents, schools and employers. It reflected — he thought — a shift in thinking from a society that judges people on their credentials to one that values people on what they become.

Consistent with his lecture's emphasis on foundations and the preparation of children for their own lives, he expressed concerns about inequalities in society that other speakers also expressed. He felt that when children from well-off families start school, they would have had an enormous advantage. Their lives would already have been enriched by various experiences. There was a danger of what might be called a hereditary meritocracy. Expanding pre-school education was one way to level up all children, regardless of their social backgrounds.

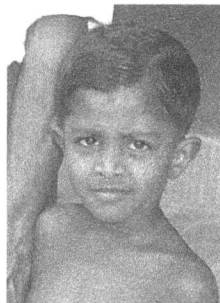

Like some other speakers, Janadas Devan protested his want of qualifications to speak about children, but his thoughtful reflection on issues of childhood and parenting definitely suggests otherwise.

Janadas Devan in 1959

The 8th Lecture, delivered 11 October 2014

I am massively unqualified to talk about children. My knowledge of the subject is defined more by what I don't know — which is enormous — than what I know, which is very little indeed. On this narrow raft, nevertheless, I propose to navigate across my own vast ocean of ignorance. Let me begin by saying a little of the title of my talk: "Your children are not your children". Whatever does that mean?

The line is of course from a poem by Kahlil Gibran, the Lebanese-American writer, in his best-known book *The Prophet.*[1] Gibran's reputation has suffered of late but *The Prophet* has never been out of print since it was first published in 1923, and has sold more than 10 million copies in about 50 different languages since then.

It consists of 26 prose poems, delivered as sermons by a wise man called Al Mustapha. He is about to set sail for his homeland after 12 years in exile on an island, when the people of the island ask him to share his wisdom on the big questions of life: love, work, family and death.

One of the poems is entitled "On Children", which reads:

> Your children are not your children.
> They are the sons and daughters of Life's longing for itself.
> They come through you but not from you,
> And though they are with you yet they belong not to you.
>
> You may give them your love but not your thoughts
> For they have their own thoughts.
> You may house their bodies but not their souls,
> For their souls dwell in the house of tomorrow which you cannot
>   visit, not even in your dreams.
> You may strive to be like them, but seek not to make them like
>   you for life goes not backward nor tarries with yesterday.
> You are the bows from which your children as living arrows are
>   sent forth.

---

[1] Kahlil Gibran, *The Prophet* (New York: AA Knopf, 1923).

The archer sees the mark upon the path of the infinite,
And He bends you with His might that His arrows may go swift
and far.
Let your bending in the archer's hand be for gladness;
For even as He loves the arrow that flies
so He loves also the bow that is stable.

Gibran was a Christian and was familiar with the paradoxical turns of mystical Christianity — like for instance those found in Saint John of the Cross' "Dark Night of the Soul":

In order to possess what you do not possess
You must go by the way of dispossession.
In order to arrive at what you are not
You must go through the way in which you are not.

and so on and so forth.

I don't particularly admire most of Gibran's work, but what he says of children has always struck me as sound advice about parenting. I felt that way when I was the child myself, not the parent, trying to find my footing beyond the shadows of my parents; and I feel it even more now that I'm a parent, trying to find my bearing as my son tries to find his own footing beyond the shadows of *his* parents.

"Your children are not your children; though they are with you yet they belong not to you." The older parents among you especially might know what I mean when I say that quite apart from raising your children properly as they are growing up — providing for them and giving them as much support as possible — one of the most difficult tasks of parenting comes when the raising is done and your children are ready to step out on their own. For it is then that you realise that the parent–child relationship can thrive into adulthood only if parents and children become friends: "You may give them your love but not your thoughts/For they have their own thoughts."

I feel that, as a society, we don't take the effort to understand how difficult it is to craft a home and to build an environment where our children can thrive. We should make it an option for women to stay home to raise their children, and pay them, because it's national service, for two years.

So pay parents to stay at home to bring up their children? I think it's a very good idea. We have these schemes in Singapore that encourage babies. Lots of incentive schemes, tax deductions, and so on. But actually the problem is not that people don't have babies. People who get married are replacing themselves. The fertility rate among married couples is actually at replacement level. The problem is that people don't get married. Rather than baby bonuses, we should have marriage bonuses. And paying the man or woman who decides to stay at home to look after the children might be worth pondering.

It is not an accident that the societies that have a dearth of babies are all socially conservative societies. It is not England or the Scandinavian countries that are facing low fertility rates. These are liberal societies. The societies that are facing low fertility rates are relatively traditional societies like Italy, Spain, Greece and Ireland. In East Asia, it is Japan, South Korea, Taiwan and Singapore. All these societies have educated women but they have not necessarily treated women equally. Any measure that equalises the relations between the sexes would probably result in higher fertility rates. Paying somebody to be a homemaker is a means of equalising the status of women. That's why I support this idea. It's ironic that everyone assumes the higher the participation rate of women in the workforce the lower the fertility rate, because actually it's the other way round. If you check the figures for the OECD countries, the higher the female participation rate in the workforce, the higher the fertility rate.

— From the Question & Answer session

Raising a child is a daunting responsibility. It is a life-long effort that nothing can prepare you for. It is astonishing that we spend hundreds of millions a year training HR managers but hardly a cent training parents and would-be parents. Universities have schools of industrial relations and business management, but no school of parenting devoted to studying and teaching parents about parenting. Why do we assume we can benefit from training for any aspect of our work, but not to deal with the umpteen difficulties of family life?

I confess that I'm often baffled by children. For instance, children often ask adults the most extraordinary questions. I remember my son, when he was aged three, stumping me with the question: "Why is water wet?" I was unable to answer because I didn't know the answer. I don't suppose there is a simple answer, but I would have liked to have known how to deal with especially curious children.

At other times they ask questions which you can't answer because you do know what the answer might be. I faced this difficulty when my son began asking what the nursery rhymes his parents hummed to him incessantly meant precisely:

> Goosey, goosey, gander,
> Where shall I wander?
> Upstairs and downstairs,
> And in my lady's chamber.

Try explaining to a six-year-old what someone wandering upstairs and downstairs, and into my lady's chamber, might be after. I would have liked to have learnt how not to lie and obfuscate to children even when you are trying perforce to protect them.

We look at our children as a source of joy on whom we lavish our love. Many parents also view their children as the key to the future, and would strive to provide them with the best opportunities to succeed and reach their fullest potential — both for the children's own good as well as that of the parents. However, this desire to give our children the best possible start in life, to ensure that they will be able to dream and become whatever they want to be, can often result in almost insurmountable expectations. Indeed, the pressures on children are increasing precisely because our expectations of them are getting higher, our ambitions for our children more outlandish.

Today, we measure how well our children are doing by how well they perform certain skills. We worry if our children cannot read by the age of four. Typically, a child learns to play a musical instrument by the age of five — the theory being that music develops mathematical and logical skills — and in all probability has already had swimming classes, gym lessons and ballet. Parents force improvements upon their children in an effort to give them a leg-up in life. The home has become "the anxiety-ridden arena of modern life".[2] We call this progress.

"Your children are not your children." Learn to let go, as popular wisdom puts it, and allow your children sufficient space to grow — and not only when they've ceased to be children but while they are growing up: allow them the freedom to dream their own dreams and follow their own distant drummer. When they fall, don't pick them up. When they make mistakes, don't cover for them. When they make for byways, off the beaten track, don't yank the chain.

---

[2]   Quoted from Arlie Russell Hochschild, *The Time Bind: When Work Becomes Home and Home Becomes Work* (New York: Metropolitan/Holt, 1997).

Many of us are ambitious for our children, perhaps inordinately so. We should not have preconceived notions of what our children should become, and impose our own ambitions on them. "Seek not to make them like you," as Gibran puts it.

Too much pressure on the child is undesirable. A child should have the time to be a child. Let children discover the wonder and marvel of life. Let them have time to play and enjoy themselves. Let them uncover their own pleasures — the joy of catching frogs in *longkangs*,[3] of climbing trees, of bicycling down steep paths at 60 mph (without a helmet).

I am not by any means advocating that parents should abandon their children to their own devices. Of course, we need to provide support, but let the support not become a straight-jacket. "You are the bows from which your children as living arrows are sent forth." The stability of the bow is absolutely necessary if the arrow is to fly "swift and far", let alone reach its mark. It is of course not an easy task trying to strike a balance between wanting to ensure the best upbringing for your children, while allowing them sufficient space to grow into unique individuals. What model of childhood should guide us? What precisely is "childhood"?

As I said at the outset, I'm singularly ill-equipped to address such questions. To begin with, I remember almost nothing of my own childhood. I remember a good many things that happened to me when I was a child, of course; I remember especially many of the things that happened around me — among my family, in the schools I attended, in Singapore. But I don't remember how it felt to be a child. What it felt like to feel as a child; what the world seemed to me when I was a child — all an utter blank! "The child is the father of the man," says William Wordsworth, and "I could wish my days to be/Bound each to each by natural piety."[4]

---

[3] Malay for "storm drains".

[4] Taken from Wordsworth's poem — "My Heart Leaps up When I Behold". In William Wordsworth, *Poems, in Two Volumes* (London: Longman, Hurst, Rees & Orme, 1807), Vol. II.

As a matter of my own brute experience, my days don't seem bound each to each by natural piety — certainly not stretching back to the days of my childhood; and far from the child being father to the man, in my case it seems more like the man is the father of the child. For when I look back on my own childhood, I interpret it in terms of the adult that I am today, and I don't recall how the child that was me felt *as a child*. I feel — I know it can't be true — but I feel as though I've always been 40!

I reassure myself that I may not be rare in this. Most people don't recall with great clarity what it felt like to be a child. Many people might have a greater recall of their own childhoods than I do of mine — and thus have greater empathy for children, their own as well of others, than I do — but I don't think I'm different from others in kind so much as in degree.

Consider for instance what a bewildering variety of views — images, assumptions, conceptions — there have been of childhood throughout history. Consider what extraordinary — bizarre, fanciful even — things that some highly intelligent people have said about childhood.

Take, for instance, what Philippe Ariès said in *Centuries of Childhood*. Published in the early 1960s, this book was influential for decades, its thesis that childhood was a modern invention widely accepted. "The idea of childhood did not exist" till the Victorian era, Ariès held.[5] Before the 16th century, there was no such thing as childhood, he declared. Before that, they were simply considered smaller, weaker and less intelligent than adults. He used the portrayal of children as miniature adults in 12th-century paintings as a supporting example.

Many scholars once adopted this view. For example, Edward Shorter writes in *The Making of the Modern Family* that "in traditional

---

[5] Phillipe Ariès, 1962, Quoted in Hugh Cunningham, "The History of Childhood", in C. Philip Hwang, Michael E. Lamb, and Irving E. Sigel, eds., *Images of Childhood*, (New York: Psychology Press, 1996), 27–24. See also Chapter 4 by Aline Wong in this volume.

society, mothers viewed the development and happiness of infants younger than two with indifference".[6] The theory was that most children, before the modern era, died young. Therefore parents did not invest any emotion in their children. Roughly a quarter of children died within a year of their birth; and about half rarely went beyond seven. Thus it became "unrewarding" — to quote the historian Barbara Tuchman — to love children.[7]

This is an extraordinary conceit. The evidence from literature alone — never mind 12th-century portraiture — does not support the theory that most adult human beings before the modern era had little feelings for their children. If this were so, it would be very difficult to explain numerous poems before the Victorian era mourning the death of children. Shakespeare himself wrote such poems — for he had a son who died in his teens. His contemporary Ben Jonson did the same — for a son who died in infancy. The death of children was thought to be as tragic in 1500 as it seems today, in every culture.

Although most scholars reject Ariès' account now, most would accept that childhood is a conceptual category — a social construction as much as it is a biological one. Our notions of childhood and conceptions of what a child should be have changed over time. Indeed, there has never been agreement on the simplest questions about childhood: "What does the word 'childhood' mean?" "How do we determine its duration?" "How long does childhood last?" "When do children cease being children?" There has never been agreement on such questions for the simple reason it is not possible to settle them by a simple appeal to biology.

At the risk of simplifying a bewildering variety of views, I would say the view of childhood in the western tradition has swung between two poles: either children were considered devils or

---

[6] Edward Shorter, 1976, as quoted by Cunningham. Ibid., 29.
[7] Barbara W. Tuchman, *A Distant Mirror: The Calamitous 14th Century*, (New York: Ballantine Books, 1978).

children were thought to be angels. It is different in various eastern traditions.

For centuries in the West, notions about childhood were inseparable from the notion of "original sin". Since on this view we are all born with original sin, children especially were innately evil. In English, sayings such as "spare the rod and spoil the child" and "only fire can straighten crooked wood" originated in the 16th and 17th centuries when Puritan ideas of childhood were dominant. Children were to be disciplined, corrected and purged; otherwise their innate propensity to do evil would not be curbed.

Take for instance James Janeway's *A Token For Children,* which was published around 1660. It is regarded as the first book written in English of children, for children. It contains extraordinary tales of pious and obedient children lying on their deathbeds, giving accounts of the sins they have committed such as idleness and inattentiveness. But due to their conversion, the dying children speak of their delight at their salvation and their happiness at the prospect of receiving their eternal reward. For instance, little Ann Greenough, who died at the age of five, is said to have "had an unspeakable delight in catechising", and "was very frequent and constant in secret prayer", with "thoughts of death wherein she took such pleasure..."[8] Imagine reading that to your child at bedtime. And yet this was among the most popular children's books in English till well into the 18th century.

Indeed, we had these kinds of books well into the 19th century. Take for instance Mary Martha Sherwood's didactic *History of the Fairchild Family,* published in three volumes between 1818 and 1847. They recount a series of lessons that the Fairchild parents taught their three children to orient their souls towards Heaven. Mary Martha Sherwood assured her readers: "All children are by nature evil, and while they have none but the natural evil principle

---

[8] "Example 4: Ann Greenough", in James Janeway, *A Token for Children, Volume 1* (London: Forgotten Books, 2013), 120–122.

to guide them, pious and prudent parents must check their naughty passions in any way that they have in their power."[9]

It is instructive to see how this idea informed even those who expressly rejected it. Take for instance the philosopher John Locke, who challenged the idea that children were innately evil and proposed instead that they were born *tabula rasa*, a blank slate. The right environment and right education could thus shape any child to become a rational and responsible being. But even Locke thought nothing of suggesting that the children of the poor be put to work from the age of three. For him as for most people up to fairly recently, everyone in the household, even children aged three, was ultimately a unit of labour.[10] The school year in America was — and remains — shaped by the needs of farming. Why do American schools have long summer breaks — roughly from May till August? Because that was when children were required to help with the harvesting.

The other image of childhood — that they were potential angels — always co-existed with the image of them as potential devils at worst or potential units of production at best. But the angelic image has been dominant over the past two centuries, especially after the Romantic era, when childhood became increasingly perceived in a positive light. Children were not merely *tabula rasa*; they were guiltless and virtuous — by nature.

Thus we find Rousseau writing in *Emile* of children being born naturally good; if they do wrong, it is only because of the corrupting influence of adults.[11] Childhood was deemed innocent; adulthood corrupt. In the English tradition, this view was best expressed by William Wordsworth. Take for instance his *Ode:*

---

[9] Mary Martha Sherwood as quoted in "The Moral Tale: (i) Didactic", in Frederick Joseph Harvey Darton, *Children's Books in England: Five Centuries of Social Life* (Cambridge: Cambridge University Press, 2011), 175.

[10] See John Locke, "An Essay on the Poor Law," in Mark Goldie ed., *Locke: Political Essays* (Cambridge: Cambridge University Press, 1997), 182–200.

[11] Jean-Jacques Rousseau, *Emile*, trans. Barbara Foxley (London: J.M. Dent & Sons, 1911).

Intimations of Immortality.[12] It is a lovely poem, thrilling in its appeal. Here are a few verses:

> There was a time when meadow, grove and stream,
> The earth, and every common sight,
>> To me did seem
>> Apparell'd in celestial light,
> The glory and the freshness of a dream.
> It is not now as it hath been of yore;
>> Turn wheresoe'er I may,
>> By night or day,
> The things which I have seen I now can see no more.

He is speaking here of how the world seemed to him when he was a child — "apparelled in celestial light". And what happens as the child becomes a boy and then a man? Well, this is how Wordsworth saw it:

> Our birth is but a sleep and a forgetting:
> The Soul that rises with us, our life's Star,
>> Hath had elsewhere its setting,
>> And cometh from afar:
>> Not in entire forgetfulness,
>> And not in utter nakedness,
> But trailing clouds of glory do we come
>> From God, who is our home:
> Heaven lies about us in our infancy!
> Shades of the prison-house begin to close
>> Upon the growing Boy,
> But he beholds the light, and whence it flows,
>> He sees it in his joy;
> The Youth, who daily farther from the east
>> Must travel, still is Nature's priest,
>> And by the vision splendid
>> Is on his way attended;

---

[12] William Wordsworth, *Ode: Intimations of Immortality from Recollections of Early Childhood* (Whitefish, MT: Literary Licensing LLC, 2014).

> At length the Man perceives it die away,
> And fade into the light of common day.

The progression from infancy to boyhood to youth to manhood is positively tragic. Shades of the prison-house — life — begin to close in soon after childhood. The boy sees a little of the light, the youth even less — till finally in adulthood, as the prison doors clang shut, we only have the light of common day, and "nothing can bring back the hour/Of splendour in the grass, of glory in the flower." Life is a forgetting of innocence.

How do you know when you're not a child anymore?

HG Wells, the famous science fiction writer, once remarked that he could never understand how a child's sense of wonder, sense of possibility and sense of adventure could turn into what so many adults become — dull, predictable and boring. He said he could never understand that. And I think it is true. If you look at children and many years later, you see what they become, actually it's more often than not a closing of possibilities rather than an opening of possibilities. The rare individual is one who remains a child for as long as possible.

— From the Question & Answer session

We are in many ways the inheritors of the Romantic tradition. The modern view of childhood is not suffused with the soft mysticism of Wordsworth, but we do generally agree with him and other Romantics, like Blake, in seeing the world of the adult as potentially corrupting of the child. Thus we have laws to protect children from sexual abuse, from pornography, from bad influences of all variety. Indeed, almost all the reforming energy of the past 150 years or so that has been devoted to improving the lives of children derives from the image of childhood that was first spawned by the Romantics. The ending of child labour, universal schooling, improvements in child nutrition — that huge machinery of nurturing, from the cradle through the nursery to the kindergarten — are essentially post-Romantic.

But the argument is by no means over. The two views — of the child as incarnate sin and the child as the incarnate lamb — repeat an old polarity that has never ended but merely morphed in various ways. It goes back in the western tradition to the 5th century in the debate that roiled the early Church, between the Augustinians and the Pelagians.

Augustine of Hippo believed the sin of Adam was inherited by all human beings — and "no one is good, not even one". The post-lapsarian world is by definition a fallen world, depraved and corrupt; and our only salvation is Grace. The Briton Pelagius, on the other hand, believed that Adam's sin affected only Adam. The world we are born into is not irredeemably fallen; and we can be saved by effort, work, as much as by Grace. The early Church ruled the Pelagian view heretical and the Augustinian orthodox.

There was a resumption of this debate in the 16th and 17th centuries. The Jansenists re-emphasised the Augustinian views of original sin, irredeemable human depravity, the necessity of Grace, and predestination. Their opponents were the Jesuits, who emphasised Will as much as Grace. This time, the Church ruled Jansenism a heresy — in large part because it resembled Calvinism in emphasising pre-destination.

The contemporary form of this ancient debate between the Augustinians and the Pelagians is that between nature and nurture, between genetics and environment. Is what you are the result of your genes — fixed, unalterable, predestined? Or is what you are the result of your environment — alterable, eminently malleable?

My own view — and this may be a cop-out — is a little of both. It seems to me beyond doubt that our genetic inheritance determines a great deal of what we can become. Obviously, with my

Growing up, what were the significant things that you can recollect?

Well, I remember a lot of things that happened when I was a child because of the nature of the family I grew up in. So I remember, for example, the 1963 general election when I was about eight or nine years old. I remember separation from Malaysia when I was about 10. So it was unusual in that sense. There is a book called *The Battle for Merger*, containing talks that the then Prime Minister Lee Kuan Yew gave in 1961. I don't remember hearing the talks, but I remember reading the book in 1964 when I was about nine and I read it because a lot of the people mentioned in the book were people I knew. And so I have those memories. But of how I felt as a child, I have no memory. I don't think I am unusual in that. Do you remember your childhood vividly? I'd be very ashamed if you did.

— From the Question & Answer session

genetic inheritance, I had no chance of being an Olympic athlete. I think I was also born with certain in-born intellectual predilections — and disabilities. For example, I'm partially colour-blind. I have very poor powers of visualisation. When I close my eyes, I can't visualise my own face, let alone yours. I have never in my life dreamt in colour. As a result of these disabilities, I did very poorly in Art. I could have spent my whole life learning to paint in the best art schools in the world, and I would never have become a passable painter, let alone a good one.

On the other hand, I seem to have inherited, partially, my father's musical gifts. I'm not a good singer, unlike my father, who had an almost concert-quality singing voice, but I have a passably good ear. I am good at scanning lines of poetry. I don't have perfect pitch, but I can get by pretty well. But also, much as I love music, I don't have preternatural musical gifts. To be able to think in terms of notes, scales, intervals, harmonies and musical themes as composers do — I can't imagine anything that would be more

How did you as a parent allow sufficient space for your children to grow into unique individuals?

My wife and I didn't want our son to become like us. Somebody who would do literature, become a writer, and teach English literature. So we did the usual things. We read to him, and so on. But I never read Wordsworth to him and we consciously did not give him a traditional literary education. He did well, he did science subjects, and he ended up in university in Chicago. He began by doing Economics. Second year he moved to Political Science because he thought Economics is a bit too boring. The third year, what does he do? He does English. So you'll understand when I say I believe in original sin and predestination, because I think there may be something very deep, genetically, that predisposes any child of mine or connected to me in those directions. The older we become the more we see ourselves reflected in our children. That's my experience. I don't know whether this is the experience of everyone.

— From the Question & Answer session

thrilling. But I'm incapable of such thought. The only music I'm occasionally capable of expressing is the music of words. I might have spent an eternity in musical conservatories and I would not have become a concert pianist or a composer of the third rank, let alone the first. I am in this sense an Augustinian — I think we are predestined by certain gifts as well as disabilities that we are born with.

But I don't think the Augustinian world view is completely right. It may be the first word, but it cannot be the last. Education, training, effort, discipline — sweat — do have a material effect on what each of us becomes. I don't think we can make a silk purse out of a sow's ear — but you can make a very good purse out of a sow's ear, whatever that is, if you try very hard. The best sow's ear purse.

You have given us a great overview of the historical western view of children. Can you briefly give us the historical Asian view?

I am not an expert, but my suspicion is you will not find these kinds of polarities — original sin and innocence — in Chinese culture. They probably are not pronounced in Indian culture either. Perhaps there is a little in Islam, simply because there is a common origin in the Abrahamic traditions. I don't know enough to speak with any kind of certainty, but I suspect that in many Asian cultures the child is not thought of independently by himself but in the context of his or her family and community. If you look at Chinese language and culture, entities are never defined by themselves. So for example, the word "Good" is actually mother and child. "Good" is defined in terms of a relationship. So instead of Wordsworth talking about the solitary children and how he experienced things, I suspect the Chinese Wordsworth would have located the child in the context of the family and the community above all.

— From the Question & Answer session

Let me end with two stories about my own father to illustrate what I think might be the balance between these two polarities.

The first is an exchange my wife had with my father about 35 years ago, about "human nature". "If you met a ferocious tiger it would be human nature to run", he told her. "But what if there was a baby between you and the tiger? It would be human nature then to rescue the baby, no matter what the consequences to you," he said. My wife was staggered by his conviction. It seemed obvious to her that human nature was not as he had described it. You read in the media every day of people sacrificing the equivalents of babies to save their own skins. My father, she concluded, thought it was human nature to rescue the baby because that was what he would have done. He had generalised his own intrinsic nature as applying to all humanity. That might explain him — the strange uncalculating courage he had — but I don't think it applies to all of us. I don't think any amount of training or nurturing is going to turn natural mice into roaring lions.

The second occurred when I was 14 or so. My father had taken his children to Raffles Lighthouse, where we stayed for a few days. There, among the rocks, he told us one afternoon about evolution. How natural selection worked. How species that adapted themselves to their environment survived; and how those that didn't, didn't. How the accumulation of random genetic variations, interacting with the environment, resulted in new species. And so on.

The lesson was conducted in a highly original fashion. Illustrations included quotations from poetry, especially Wordsworth. There were digressions. He told us of Shiva-Nataraja, the Lord of the Dance, holding in one hand the drum that summoned existence into being, and, in the other, the fire that destroyed it — and how both, creation and destruction, were part of one universal process. And then he said something I will never forget, for it expressed his deepest belief. It was no longer science — it was religion.

"For life to have emerged from matter, matter must have had the potential for life," he said. "And for consciousness to have emerged from life, life must have had the potential for consciousness. And for human ideals to have emerged from consciousness, consciousness must have had the potential for those ideals. We wouldn't dream unless those dreams are capable of fulfilment. It is not what you are that matters; it is what you can become. That process never ends."

I believe that. What model of childhood should we be guided by? I don't know, but whatever it is, it should not be governed by a limiting vision of what the child is but rather by what the child can become. I don't like tests and assessments, necessary as they are, for this reason; they can only tell you what people did, not what they can do. It is becoming — what you can become — that matters; not what you began with. I believe in both original sin and innocence — and the endless possibility of grace and redemption.

Janadas Devan (right) with his parents and younger brother Janamitra, June 1959. Mr Nair had just been released from political detention following the victory of the People's Action Party in the 1959 General Election.

Source: *The Straits Times* © Singapore Press Holdings Limited. Reprinted with permission.

You ended up saying that it is what you can become that is important. So you reopened the pressures that parents experience to make their child become the most, and we are back to the very problem that you decried at the start, which is "You shouldn't be trying to guide and pressure your children so much." So isn't there some contradiction there?

Yes, there is some contradiction, but I think what we have is a system, and perhaps it's difficult to imagine a different system, which measures people by what they start with. We are the only country in the world that confers the title of "scholar" on people at the age of 18, on the basis of how well they did in A Levels. Every other country confers the title of "scholar" on people who have written at least 10 books and when they are 80 years old. When you give a scholarship, and you have to give scholarships, you don't make a decision based on what you think somebody is capable of becoming. You base it on what they have already done.

Now you must have heard the Prime Minister speak about ASPIRE in the National Day Rally. ASPIRE is essentially an effort to shift society from an overemphasis on what people did, to what they can become. I don't think it's going to be an easy shift, not least because for better or worse we have inherited an elitist culture. The word Mandarin originates from Chinese culture. They had this examination system for centuries to determine who was going to be the scholar working for the emperor and what grade he worked in. We inherited the Chinese tradition. The Brahmin tradition in India is just as elitist. On top of this cultural inheritance, our colonial masters were among the most elitist of the colonial powers, exceeded only, perhaps, by the French. So we have inherited the worst of all worlds and we have perpetuated it. So this transition is going to be very difficult, but I think it's a transition that we have to make.

Should the education of a child have the rigour that gives them discipline to fulfil their potential or the openness that allows them to find their potential? There is a quote from Seneca: "To a ship without direction, no wind is favourable." How do we reconcile these two necessities for success?

Alfred North Whitehead, the philosopher and mathematician, wrote a short essay in which he spoke about the natural rhythms of education. He said there are three stages in any education process. The first is the stage of Romance. This is when people discover the new, the exciting. But you can't go through life being excited by things. You have to buckle down and learn, which he called the second stage, the stage of Discipline. Romance is important. It's the stage of wonder. But discipline and rigour, to use your words, are equally important. And it's only after you have gone through the second stage that you can arrive at the third, which Whitehead called Generalisation. This is wonder and romance again, but at a higher level.

I don't think you go through one stage after another in sequence. Probably a number of stages are involved at once. But you can see the aptness of Whitehead's characterisation in the way children grow up. I can still remember how my son suddenly realised how words, when combined, make something new, and it was significant. It was a sudden discovery. I remember observing him. It's a sudden stage of empowerment. But after that you really have to learn how to spell. You have to sit down and memorise your words; you have to memorise your multiplication tables, and so on. You have to do both — encourage wonder and romance as well as discipline.

One of the worst things is to insist on "either/or" formulations. The world is complex; there are probably more than two things involved in any one issue.

— From the Question & Answer session

Thank you for sharing so poetically. You said it's essential for parents to learn about parenthood, but most of us stumble into that journey unprepared and unqualified. How can we learn?

It's astonishing that we do so little preparation. The People's Association occasionally organises parenting classes. Most of us depend on churches, temples, grandparents, and so on. But societies that have tried to solve this problem have gone to extremes. In communist China in the 1950s, Mao organised the entire country into communes and children were taken away from their parents. They were brought up by the communes, by the state. *Brave New World* was a dystopian vision that Aldous Huxley had of the future: taking children away from their parents and having the state raise the children scientifically. You hear the phrase, "It takes a village to raise a child." I'm not so sure. Perhaps it doesn't take a village; it takes a family. But there has to be some means struck between family at one end with all its quirks and sometimes disabilities, and the state stepping in. There has to be some kind of balance between the two and I don't think any society has quite found that balance yet.

— From the Question & Answer session

The Book Committee

To mark the nation's Jubilee celebrations, the Singapore Children's Society determined to compile the Society's annual public lectures into a book. A Book Committee led by Associate Professor John Elliott was formed to manage the project. The work involved collating and editing the eight lectures to a common book style, while retaining their essence and nuances. It also entailed interviews with the speakers for their post-lecture reflections and the sourcing for images and illustrations. Mr Morgan Chua, one of Singapore's best-known cartoonists, was commissioned to produce a cartoon for each of the chapters. The Committee was also responsible for overseeing the publication of the book.

Book Committee Members

John Elliott (Chair) — Associate Professor, Department of Psychology, NUS, and longstanding volunteer with the Singapore Children's Society. He also chairs the Society's Research Committee and is a member of its Executive Committee.

Mae-Lim Hoon Ann — Contract Liaison Officer with the Singapore Ministry of Foreign Affairs. A nurse by profession, she was the Honorary Secretary of the Singapore Children's Society from 1987 to 2014 and is a member of the Society's Research and Advocacy Standing Committee and Sunbeam Place Standing Committee.

Alfred Tan — Chief Executive Officer, Singapore Children's Society. He is head of agency since 1999.

Sue Cheng — Senior Director, Research & Outreach Centre, Singapore Children's Society. She was recruited as a Senior Counsellor in 2002.

Lin Xiaoling — Assistant Director, Public Education & Advocacy, Singapore Children's Society. She is a staff member since 2010.

Grace Yap — Public Education Executive, Singapore Children's Society. She is a staff member since 2013.

Index

www.ingramcontent.com/pod-product-compliance
Lightning Source LLC
Chambersburg PA
CBHW050648280326
41932CB00015B/2820